W9-BGK-346

# MAPS OF THE WORLD

## Volume 3: U.S. Physical Atlas

# Introduction & Acknowledgments

## *Introduction*

The maps in this volume present a picture of the physical geography of the United States. Together they provide a detailed view of our nation's natural world, including:

- the shape of the land and bodies of water
- the climate
- phenomena such as earthquakes and glaciers
- the natural vegetation that grows on the Earth as well as the minerals that lie beneath its surface.

This physical atlas also includes maps that show how human beings have interacted with the physical environment. There are maps locating where crops and animals are raised as well as places where people have created parks and transportation routes.

To show this wide range of information the mapmakers have created a variety of maps. Some use symbols and labels to locate minerals or parks or highways. On *isobar maps* lines connect similar areas—places in which rainfall or temperature are the same, for example. *Choropleth maps* use areas of color to indicate information such as where corn or cows are raised. The MapSkills section that appears on pages 63–78 of this volume is a useful guide to different kinds of maps and how to read them.

Published by Grolier Educational


For information, address the publisher:
Grolier Educational, Danbury, CT 06816

***Library of Congress Cataloging-in-Publication Data***

Grolier Educational (Firm)
Maps of the world.
p. cm.
Includes index.
Contents: v. 1. Glossary of map terms -- v. 2. U.S. political atlas -- v. 3. U.S. physical atlas -- v. 4. U.S. cultural atlas -- v. 5. World political atlas: Africa and Asia -- v. 6. World political atlas: Australia and Europe -- v. 7. World political atlas: North America and South America -- v. 8. World physical atlas -- v. 9. World cultural atlas -- v. 10. U.S. and world history atlas.
ISBN 0-7172-7662-7 (set)
1. Children atlases. [1. Atlases.] I. Title.
G1021 .G6865 1997 <G&M>
912--DC21 97-5074
CIP
MAPS

***Acknowledgments***
Cover: Smart Graphics

MapSkills authors: Susan Buckley and Elspeth Leacock
MapSkills research and design (GeoSystems):
Debbie Freer, Luis Freile, Brian Goudreau, Andy Green, Jeannine Schonta, Andy Skinner



Printed and bound in the United States of America

# Contents

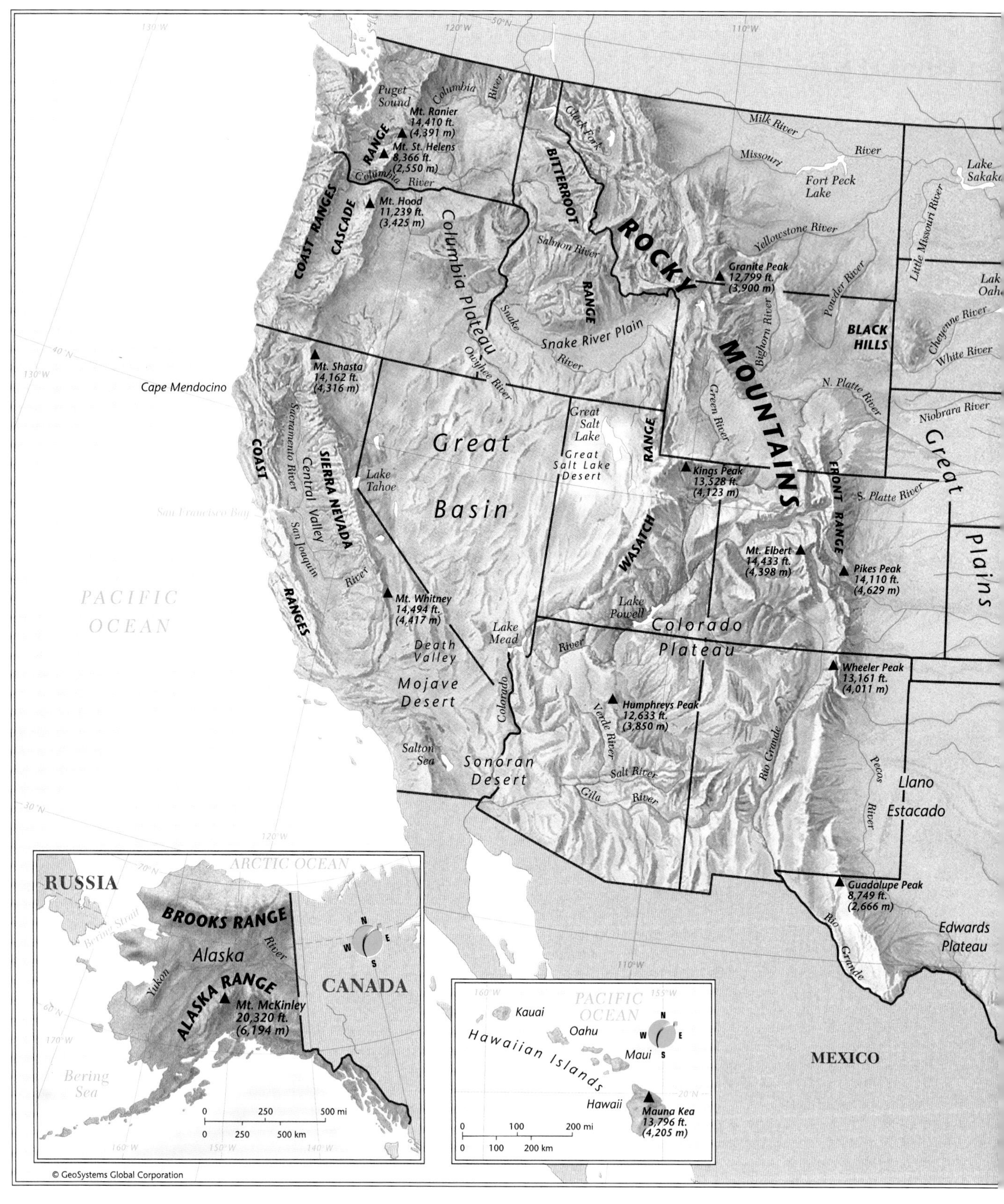

Puget Sound
Columbia River
Mt. Ranier 14,410 ft. (4,391 m)
Mt. St. Helens 8,366 ft. (2,550 m)
RANGE
Columbia River
Mt. Hood 11,239 ft. (3,425 m)
COAST RANGES
CASCADE
Columbia Plateau
Clark Fork
BITTERROOT
RANGE
Salmon River
Snake
ROCKY
MOUNTAINS
Milk River
Missouri River
Fort Peck Lake
Yellowstone River
Granite Peak 12,799 ft. (3,900 m)
Powder River
Bighorn River
Little Missouri River
Lake Sakakawea
Lake Oahe
BLACK HILLS
Cheyenne River
White River
Snake River Plain
Snake River
Owyhee River
Mt. Shasta 14,162 ft. (4,316 m)
Cape Mendocino
N. Platte River
Niobrara River
Green River
Great Salt Lake
Great Salt Lake Desert
RANGE
Great Basin
Lake Tahoe
COAST
Sacramento River
Central Valley
SIERRA NEVADA
San Francisco Bay
San Joaquin River
Kings Peak 13,528 ft. (4,123 m)
FRONT RANGE
S. Platte River
Great Plains
WASATCH
Mt. Elbert 14,433 ft. (4,398 m)
Pikes Peak 14,110 ft. (4,629 m)
PACIFIC OCEAN
RANGES
Mt. Whitney 14,494 ft. (4,417 m)
Lake Powell
Colorado Plateau
Lake Mead
River
Death Valley
Mojave Desert
Colorado
Wheeler Peak 13,161 ft. (4,011 m)
Humphreys Peak 12,633 ft. (3,850 m)
Verde River
Salton Sea
Sonoran Desert
Salt River
Gila River
Rio Grande
Pecos River
Llano Estacado
Guadalupe Peak 8,749 ft. (2,666 m)
Rio Grande
Edwards Plateau
MEXICO
RUSSIA
ARCTIC OCEAN
BROOKS RANGE
Bering Strait
Alaska
River
Yukon
ALASKA RANGE
Mt. McKinley 20,320 ft. (6,194 m)
CANADA
Bering Sea
0 250 500 mi
0 250 500 km
PACIFIC OCEAN
Kauai
Oahu
Hawaiian Islands
Maui
Hawaii
Mauna Kea 13,796 ft. (4,205 m)
0 100 200 mi
0 100 200 km
N
S
E
W

CANADA
Lake of the Woods
Lake Superior
Lake Michigan
Lake Huron
Lake Ontario
Lake Erie
MESABI RANGE
Central Lowland
Ozark Plateau
BOSTON MTS.
OUACHITA MOUNTAINS
FLINT HILLS
ADIRONDACK MTS.
GREEN MTS.
WHITE MTS.
Mt. Washington 6,288 ft. (1,917 m)
Allegheny Plateau
APPALACHIAN MOUNTAINS
ALLEGHENY MOUNTAINS
BLUE RIDGE
Mt. Mitchell 6,684 ft. (2,037 m)
Cumberland Plateau
Piedmont
Atlantic Coastal Plain
Gulf Coastal Plain
Cape Cod
Long Island
Delaware Bay
Chesapeake Bay
Cape Hatteras
ATLANTIC OCEAN
Mobile Bay
Mississippi Delta
Galveston Bay
Gulf of Mexico
Lake Okeechobee
Florida Keys
Straits of Florida
THE BAHAMAS
Red River of the North
Minnesota River
St. Croix River
Mississippi River
Wisconsin River
James River
Iowa River
Cedar River
Des Moines River
Loup R.
Platte River
Missouri River
Republican R.
Kansas River
Smoky Hill R
Arkansas River
Illinois River
Wabash River
White River
Ohio River
Kentucky R.
Green River
Cumberland River
Tennessee River
Scioto River
Grand River
Allegheny R.
Genesee River
Susquehanna River
Delaware River
Hudson River
Connecticut River
Merrimack River
Penobscot River
Saint John River
St. Lawrence River
Potomac River
James River
Roanoke River
Pee Dee R.
Savannah River
Oconee River
Ocmulgee River
Altamaha River
Flint River
Chattahoochee River
Alabama River
Tombigbee River
Pearl River
Yazoo River
Ouachita
Red River
Sabine River
Trinity River
Brazos River
Colorado River
Nueces River
Cimarron River
Canadian River
St. Johns River
90°W
80°W
70°W
50°N
40°N
30°N
N
S
E
W
0 150 300 mi
0 150 300 km
© GeoSystems Global Corporation

## State Statistics

| State | Land Area and Rank | | Geographic Center |
|---|---|---|---|
| **Alabama** | 50,750 sq mi<br>131,443 sq km | 28th | Chilton County: 12 miles southwest of Clanton |
| **Alaska** | 570,374 sq mi<br>1,477,268 sq km | 1st | 60 miles northwest of Mt. McKinley |
| **Arizona** | 113,642 sq mi<br>294,334 sq km | 6th | Yavapai County: 55 miles east-southeast of Prescott |
| **Arkansas** | 52,075 sq mi<br>134,875 sq km | 27th | Pulaski County: 12 miles northwest of Little Rock |
| **California** | 155,973 sq mi<br>403,970 sq km | 3rd | Madera County: 38 miles east of Madera |
| **Colorado** | 103,730 sq mi<br>268,660 sq km | 8th | Park County: 30 miles northwest of Pikes Peak |
| **Connecticut** | 4,845 sq mi<br>12,550 sq km | 48th | Hartford County: at East Berlin |
| **Delaware** | 1,955 sq mi<br>5,063 sq km | 49th | Kent County: 11 miles south of Dover |
| **Florida** | 53,997 sq mi<br>139,852 sq km | 26th | Hernando County: 12 miles north-northwest of Brooksville |
| **Georgia** | 57,919 sq mi<br>150,010 sq km | 21st | Twiggs County: 18 miles southeast of Macon |
| **Hawaii** | 6,423 sq mi<br>16,637 sq km | 47th | 20°15'N, 156°20'W; off Maui island |
| **Idaho** | 82,751 sq mi<br>214,325 sq km | 11th | Custer County: at Custer, southwest of Challis |
| **Illinois** | 55,593 sq mi<br>143,987 sq km | 24th | Logan County: 28 miles northeast of Springfield |
| **Indiana** | 35,870 sq mi<br>92,904 sq km | 38th | Boone County: 14 miles north-northwest of Indianapolis |
| **Iowa** | 55,875 sq mi<br>144,716 sq km | 23rd | Story County: 5 miles northeast of Ames |
| **Kansas** | 81,823 sq mi<br>211,922 sq km | 13th | Barton County: 15 miles northeast of Great Bend |
| **Kentucky** | 39,732 sq mi<br>102,907 sq km | 36th | Marion County: 3 miles north-northwest of Lebanon |
| **Louisiana** | 43,566 sq mi<br>112,836 sq km | 33rd | Avoyelles County: 3 miles southeast of Marksville |
| **Maine** | 30,865 sq mi<br>79,939 sq km | 39th | Piscataquis County: 18 miles north of Dover |
| **Maryland** | 9,775 sq mi<br>25,316 sq km | 42nd | Prince Georges County: 4½ miles northwest of Davidsonville |
| **Massachusetts** | 7,838 sq mi<br>20,300 sq km | 45th | Worcester County: north part of the City of Worcester |
| **Michigan** | 56,809 sq mi<br>147,135 sq km | 22nd | Wexford County: 5 miles north-northwest of Cadillac |
| **Minnesota** | 79,617 sq mi<br>206,207 sq km | 14th | Crow Wing County: 10 miles southwest of Brainerd |
| **Mississippi** | 46,914 sq mi<br>121,506 sq km | 31st | Leake County: 9 miles west-northwest of Carthage |
| **Missouri** | 68,898 sq mi<br>178,446 sq km | 18th | Miller County: 20 miles southwest of Jefferson City |

| Highest Point | | Lowest Point | | Temperature Maximum | Temperature Minimum | Annual Precipitation Maximum | Annual Precipitation Minimum |
|---|---|---|---|---|---|---|---|
| Cheaha Mtn. | 2,405 ft | Gulf of Mexico | Sea level | 112° | –27° | 106.57" | 22.00" |
| Mt. McKinley | 20,320 ft | Pacific Ocean | Sea level | 100° | –80° | 332.29" | 1.61" |
| Humphreys Peak | 12,633 ft | Colorado River in Yuma County | 70 ft | 128° | –40° | 58.92" | 0.07" |
| Magazine Mtn. | 2,753 ft | Ouachita River in Ashley & Union Cos. | 55 ft | 120° | –29° | 98.55" | 19.11" |
| Mt. Whitney | 14,494 ft | Death Valley | –282 ft | 134° | –45° | 153.54" | 0.00" |
| Mt. Elbert | 14,433 ft | Arkansas River in Prowers Co. | 3,350 ft | 118° | –61° | 92.84" | 1.69" |
| south slope of Mt. Frissell | 2,380 ft | Long Island Sound | Sea level | 105° | –32° | 78.53" | 23.60" |
| Ebright Road at DE-PA border | 448 ft | Atlantic Ocean | Sea level | 110° | –17° | 72.75" | 21.38" |
| Sec. 30, T.6N, R.20W in Walton Co. | 345 ft | Atlantic Ocean | Sea level | 109° | –2° | 112.43" | 21.16" |
| Brasstown Bald | 4,784 ft | Atlantic Ocean | Sea level | 112° | –17° | 112.16" | 17.14" |
| Pu'u Wekiu, Mauna Kea | 13,796 ft | Pacific Ocean | Sea level | 100° | 12° | 704.83" | 0.19" |
| Borah Peak | 12,662 ft | Snake River in Nez Perce Co. | 710 ft | 118° | –60° | 81.05" | 2.09" |
| Charles Mound | 1,235 ft | Mississippi River in Alexander Co. | 279 ft | 117° | –35° | 74.58" | 16.59" |
| Franklin Township in Wayne County | 1,257 ft | Ohio River in Posey Co. | 320 ft | 116° | –35° | 97.38" | 18.67" |
| Sec. 29, T.100N, R.41W in Osceola Co. | 1,670 ft | Mississippi River in Lee County | 480 ft | 118° | –47° | 74.50" | 12.11" |
| Mt. Sunflower | 4,039 ft | Verdigris River in Montgomery Co. | 679 ft | 121° | –40° | 67.02" | 4.77" |
| Black Mtn. | 4,139 ft | Mississippi River in Fulton Co. | 257 ft | 114° | –34° | 79.68" | 14.51" |
| Driskill Mtn. | 535 ft | New Orleans | –8 ft | 114° | –16° | 113.74" | 26.44" |
| Mt. Katahdin | 5,267 ft | Atlantic Ocean | Sea level | 105° | –48° | 75.64" | 23.06" |
| Backbone Mtn. | 3,360 ft | Atlantic Ocean | Sea level | 109° | –40° | 72.59" | 17.76" |
| Mt. Greylock | 3,487 ft | Atlantic Ocean | Sea level | 107° | –35° | 72.19" | 21.76" |
| Mt. Arvon | 1,979 ft | Lake Erie | 571 ft | 112° | –51° | 64.01" | 15.64" |
| Eagle Mtn. | 2,301 ft | Lake Superior | 600 ft | 114° | –59° | 51.53" | 7.81" |
| Woodall Mtn. | 806 ft | Gulf of Mexico | Sea level | 115° | –19° | 104.36" | 25.97" |
| Taum Sauk Mtn. | 1,772 ft | St. Francis River in Dunklin Co. | 230 ft | 118° | –40° | 92.77" | 16.14" |

## State Statistics

| State | Land Area and Rank | | Geographic Center |
|---|---|---|---|
| Montana | 145,556 sq mi<br>376,991 sq km | 4th | Fergus County: 11 miles west of Lewistown |
| Nebraska | 76,878 sq mi<br>199,113 sq km | 15th | Custer County: 10 miles northwest of Broken Bow |
| Nevada | 109,806 sq mi<br>284,397 sq km | 7th | Lander County: 26 miles southeast of Austin |
| New Hampshire | 8,969 sq mi<br>23,231 sq km | 44th | Belknap County: 3 miles east of Ashland |
| New Jersey | 7,419 sq mi<br>19,215 sq km | 46th | Mercer County: 5 miles southeast of Trenton |
| New Mexico | 121,365 sq mi<br>314,334 sq km | 5th | Torrance County: 12 miles south-southwest of Willard |
| New York | 47,224 sq mi<br>122,310 sq km | 30th | Madison County: 12 miles south of Oneida and 26 miles southwest of Utica |
| North Carolina | 48,718 sq mi<br>126,180 sq km | 29th | Chatham County: 10 miles northwest of Sanford |
| North Dakota | 68,994 sq mi<br>178,695 sq km | 17th | Sheridan County: 5 miles southwest of McClusky |
| Ohio | 40,953 sq mi<br>106,067 sq km | 35th | Delaware County: 25 miles north-northeast of Columbus |
| Oklahoma | 68,679 sq mi<br>177,878 sq km | 19th | Oklahoma County: 8 miles north of Oklahoma City |
| Oregon | 96,003 sq mi<br>248,647 sq km | 10th | Crook County: 25 miles south-southeast of Prineville |
| Pennsylvania | 44,820 sq mi<br>116,083 sq km | 32nd | Centre County: 2½ miles southwest of Bellefonte |
| Rhode Island | 1,045 sq mi<br>2,707 sq km | 50th | Kent County: 1 mile south-southwest of Crompton |
| South Carolina | 30,111 sq mi<br>77,988 sq km | 40th | Richland County: 13 miles southeast of Columbia |
| South Dakota | 75,891 sq mi<br>196,575 sq km | 16th | Hughes County: 8 miles northeast of Pierre |
| Tennessee | 41,220 sq mi<br>106,759 sq km | 34th | Rutherford County: 5 miles northeast of Murfreesboro |
| Texas | 261,914 sq mi<br>678,358 sq km | 2nd | McCulloch County: 15 miles northeast of Brady |
| Utah | 82,168 sq mi<br>212,816 sq km | 12th | Sanpete County: 3 miles north of Manti |
| Vermont | 9,249 sq mi<br>23,956 sq km | 43rd | Washington County: 3 miles east of Roxbury |
| Virginia | 35,598 sq mi<br>102,558 sq km | 37th | Buckingham County: 5 miles southwest of Buckingham |
| Washington | 66,582 sq mi<br>172,447 sq km | 20th | Chelan County: 10 miles west-southwest of Wenatchee |
| West Virginia | 24,087 sq mi<br>62,384 sq km | 41st | Braxton County: 4 miles east of Sutton |
| Wisconsin | 54,314 sq mi<br>104,673 sq km | 25th | Wood County: 9 miles southeast of Marshfield |
| Wyoming | 97,105 sq mi<br>251,501 sq km | 9th | Fremont County: 58 miles east-northeast of Lander |

| Highest Point | | Lowest Point | | Temperature Maximum | Temperature Minimum | Annual Precipitation Maximum | Annual Precipitation Minimum |
|---|---|---|---|---|---|---|---|
| Granite Peak | 12,799 ft | Kootenai River in Lincoln Co. | 1,800 ft | 117° | –70° | 55.51" | 2.97" |
| Johnson Township in Kimball County | 5,424 ft | Missouri River in Richardson Co. | 840 ft | 118° | –47° | 64.52" | 6.30" |
| Boundary Peak | 13,140 ft | Colorado River in Clark Co. | 479 ft | 125° | –50° | 59.03" | Trace |
| Mt. Washington | 6,288 ft | Atlantic Ocean | Sea level | 106° | –46° | 130.14" | 22.31" |
| High Point | 1,803 ft | Atlantic Ocean | Sea level | 110° | –34° | 85.99" | 19.85" |
| Wheeler Peak | 13,161 ft | Red Bluff Reservoir | 2,842 ft | 122° | –50° | 62.45" | 1.00" |
| Mt. Marcy | 5,344 ft | Atlantic Ocean | Sea level | 108° | –52° | 82.06" | 17.64" |
| Mt. Mitchell | 6,684 ft | Atlantic Ocean | Sea level | 110° | –34° | 129.60" | 22.69" |
| White Butte | 3,506 ft | Red River in Pembina Co. | 750 ft | 121° | –60° | 37.98" | 4.02" |
| Campbell Hill | 1,549 ft | Ohio River in Hamilton Co. | 455 ft | 113° | –39° | 70.82" | 16.96" |
| Black Mesa | 4,973 ft | Little River in McCurtain Co. | 289 ft | 120° | –27° | 84.47" | 6.53" |
| Mt. Hood | 11,239 ft | Pacific Ocean | Sea level | 119° | –54° | 168.88" | 3.33" |
| Mt. Davis | 3,213 ft | Delaware River in Delaware Co. | Sea level | 111° | –42° | 81.64" | 15.71" |
| Jerimoth Hill | 812 ft | Atlantic Ocean | Sea level | 104° | –23° | 70.21" | 24.08" |
| Sassafras Mtn. | 3,560 ft | Atlantic Ocean | Sea level | 111° | –19° | 101.65" | 20.73" |
| Harney Peak | 7,242 ft | Big Stone Lake | 966 ft | 120° | –58° | 48.42" | 2.89" |
| Clingmans Dome | 6,643 ft | Mississippi River in Shelby Co. | 178 ft | 113° | –32° | 114.88" | 25.23" |
| Guadalupe Peak | 8,749 ft | Gulf of Mexico | Sea level | 120° | –23° | 109.38" | 1.64" |
| Kings Peak | 13,528 ft | Beaverdam Wash in Washington Co. | 2,000 ft | 117° | –69° | 108.54" | 1.34" |
| Mt. Mansfield | 4,393 ft | Lake Champlain | 95 ft | 105° | –50° | 92.88" | 22.98" |
| Mt. Rogers | 5,729 ft | Atlantic Ocean | Sea level | 110° | –30° | 81.78" | 12.52" |
| Mt. Rainier | 14,410 ft | Pacific Ocean | Sea level | 118° | –48° | 184.56" | 2.61" |
| Spruce Knob | 4,861 ft | Potomac River in Jefferson Co. | 240 ft | 112° | –37° | 94.01" | 9.50" |
| Timms Hill | 1,951 ft | Lake Michigan | 579 ft | 114° | –54° | 62.07" | 12.00" |
| Gannett Peak | 13,804 ft | Belle Fourche River in Crook County | 3,099 ft | 114° | –63° | 55.46" | 1.28" |

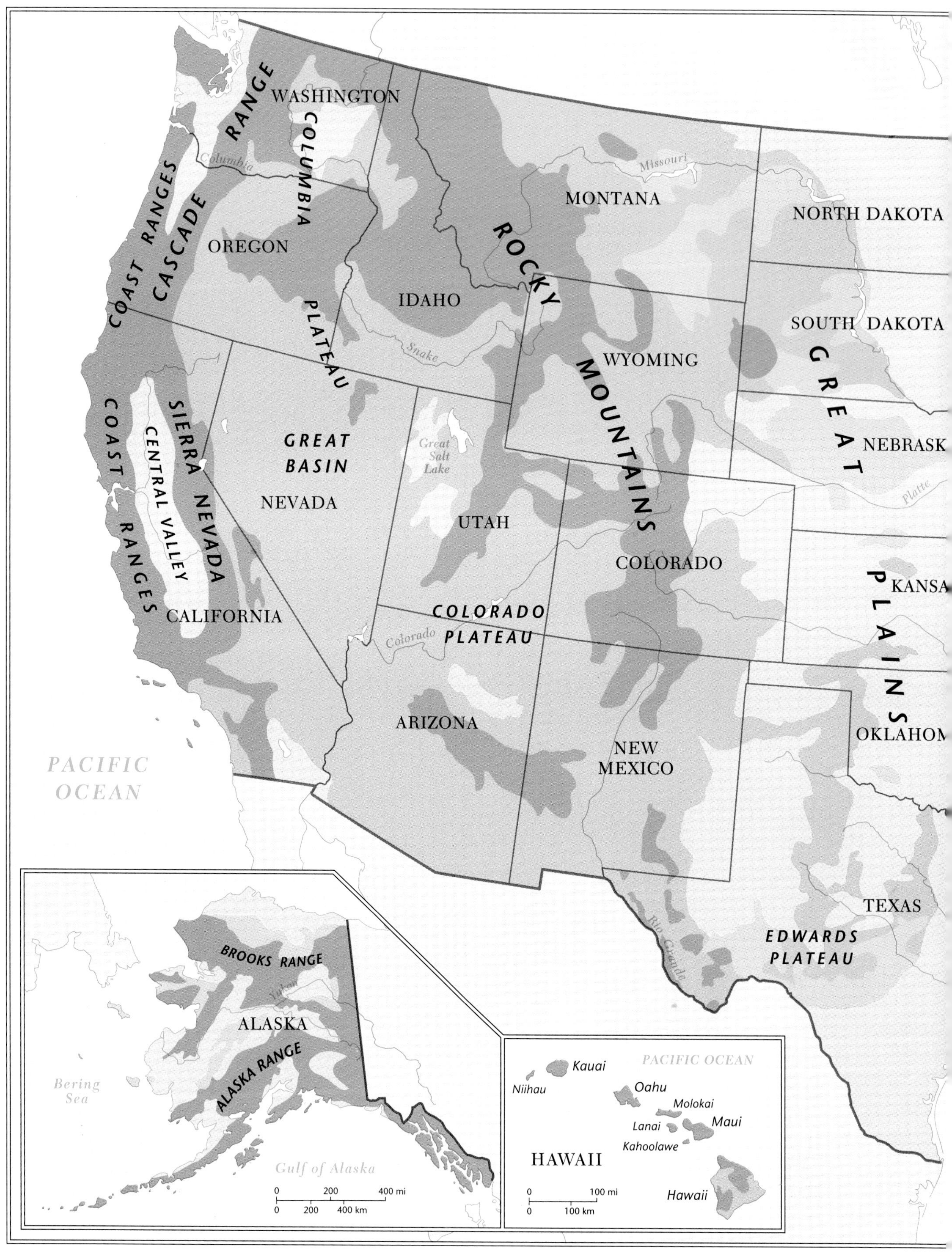
WASHINGTON
CASCADE RANGE
COLUMBIA PLATEAU
COAST RANGES
Columbia
OREGON
IDAHO
Snake
MONTANA
Missouri
NORTH DAKOTA
SOUTH DAKOTA
ROCKY MOUNTAINS
WYOMING
NEBRASK
GREAT PLAINS
Platte
GREAT BASIN
NEVADA
SIERRA NEVADA
CENTRAL VALLEY
COAST RANGES
Great Salt Lake
UTAH
COLORADO
KANSA
CALIFORNIA
COLORADO PLATEAU
Colorado
ARIZONA
NEW MEXICO
OKLAHOM
PACIFIC OCEAN
TEXAS
Rio Grande
EDWARDS PLATEAU
BROOKS RANGE
Yukon
ALASKA
ALASKA RANGE
Bering Sea
Gulf of Alaska
0 200 400 mi
0 200 400 km
Kauai
Niihau
PACIFIC OCEAN
Oahu
Molokai
Lanai
Maui
Kahoolawe
HAWAII
Hawaii
0 100 mi
0 100 km

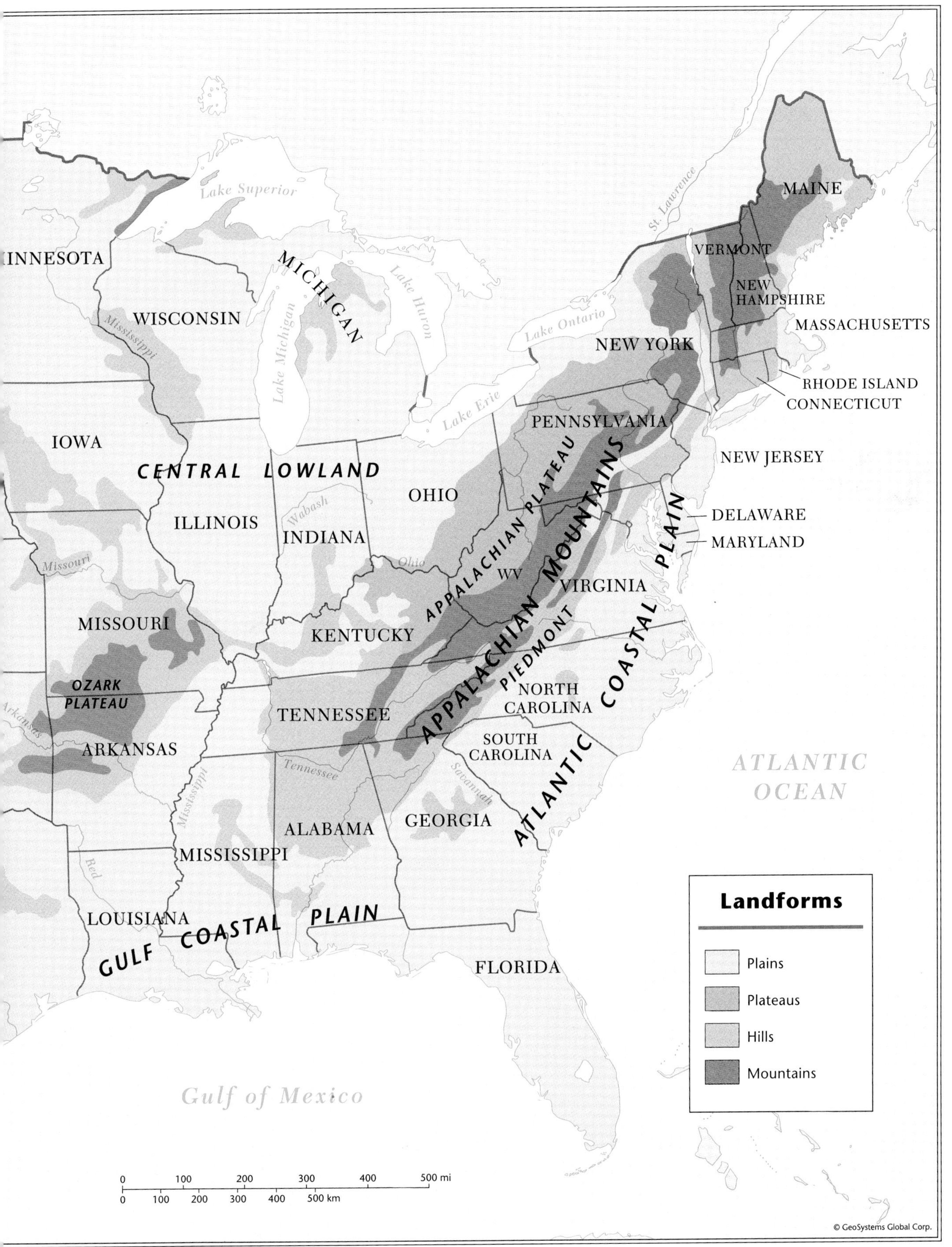
Lake Superior
St. Lawrence
MAINE
INNESOTA
MICHIGAN
Lake Huron
VERMONT
NEW HAMPSHIRE
WISCONSIN
Mississippi
Lake Michigan
Lake Ontario
MASSACHUSETTS
NEW YORK
RHODE ISLAND
CONNECTICUT
Lake Erie
PENNSYLVANIA
IOWA
NEW JERSEY
CENTRAL LOWLAND
OHIO
Wabash
APPALACHIAN PLATEAU
APPALACHIAN MOUNTAINS
ILLINOIS
DELAWARE
INDIANA
MARYLAND
Missouri
Ohio
WV
VIRGINIA
MISSOURI
KENTUCKY
APPALACHIAN
PIEDMONT
ATLANTIC COASTAL PLAIN
OZARK PLATEAU
NORTH CAROLINA
TENNESSEE
Arkansas
ARKANSAS
SOUTH CAROLINA
ATLANTIC OCEAN
Tennessee
Savannah
Mississippi
ALABAMA
GEORGIA
MISSISSIPPI
Red
LOUISIANA
GULF COASTAL PLAIN
FLORIDA
Landforms
Plains
Plateaus
Hills
Mountains
Gulf of Mexico
0 100 200 300 400 500 mi
0 100 200 300 400 500 km
© GeoSystems Global Corp.

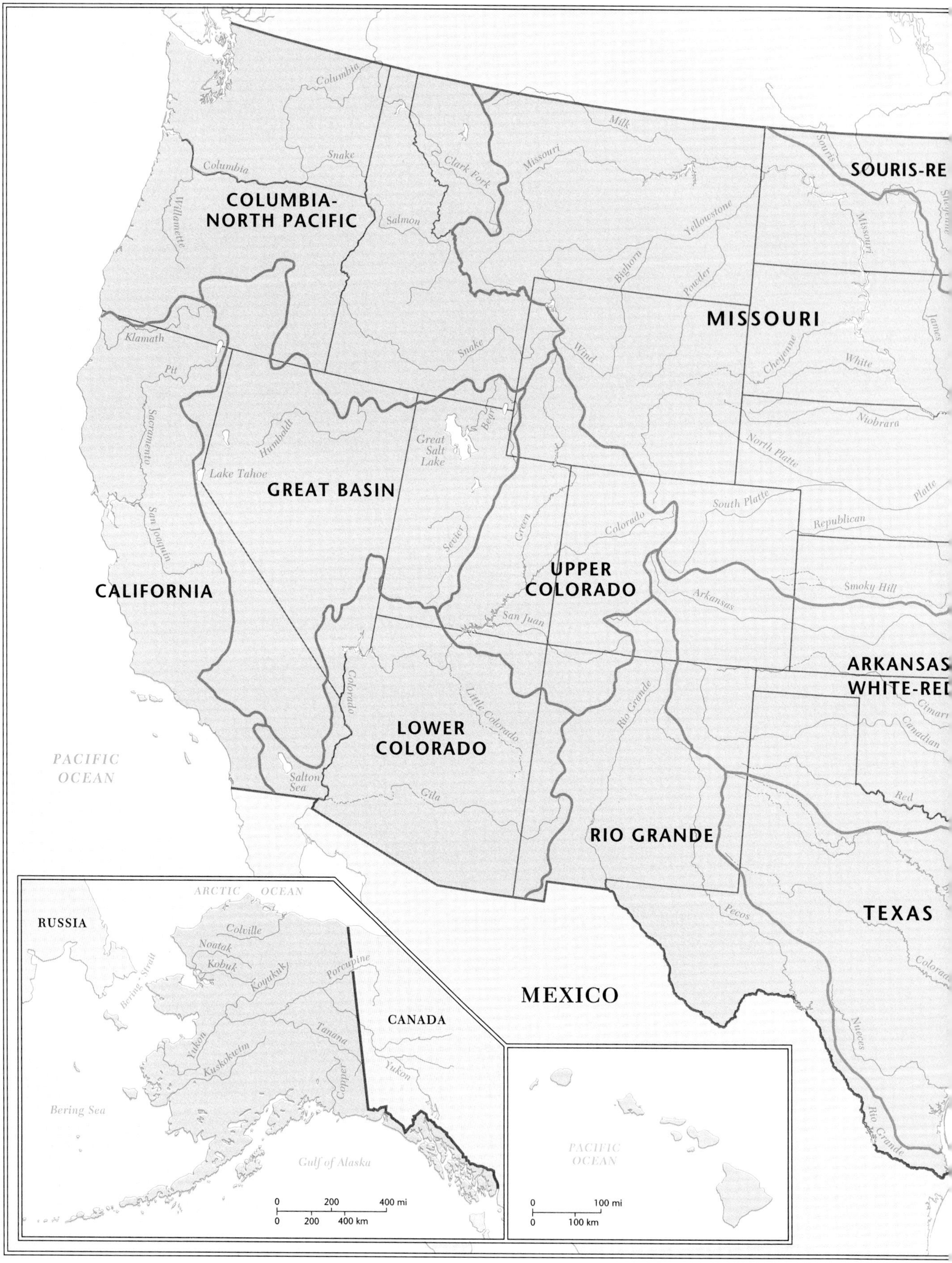

COLUMBIA-
NORTH PACIFIC

MISSOURI

SOURIS-RE

GREAT BASIN

CALIFORNIA

UPPER
COLORADO

LOWER
COLORADO

RIO GRANDE

ARKANSAS
WHITE-RE

TEXAS

MEXICO

PACIFIC
OCEAN

Columbia
Snake
Columbia
Willamette
Salmon
Clark Fork
Missouri
Milk
Yellowstone
Bighorn
Powder
Souris
Missouri
James
Klamath
Pit
Sacramento
San Joaquin
Snake
Wind
Cheyenne
White
Niobrara
North Platte
Platte
South Platte
Republican
Smoky Hill
Humboldt
Bear
Great
Salt
Lake
Lake Tahoe
Sevier
Green
Colorado
Arkansas
San Juan
Colorado
Little Colorado
Rio Grande
Cimarr
Canadian
Red
Salton
Sea
Gila
Pecos
Colorad
Nueces
Rio Grande

ARCTIC OCEAN
RUSSIA
Colville
Noatak
Kobuk
Koyukuk
Porcupine
Bering Strait
Tanana
CANADA
Yukon
Kuskokwim
Copper
Yukon
Bering Sea
Gulf of Alaska

0 200 400 mi
0 200 400 km

PACIFIC
OCEAN

0 100 mi
0 100 km

CANADA
Lake of the Woods
Rainy
AINY
Lake Superior
St. Lawrence
St. John
Lake Huron
Lake Ontario
Lake Michigan
GREAT LAKES
Connecticut
Hudson
Minnesota
Mississippi
UPPER MISSISSIPPI
Grand
Lake Erie
Wisconsin
Allegheny
Susquehanna
Delaware
Cedar
Iowa
Rock
Des Moines
NORTH ATLANTIC
Monongahela
Potomac
Illinois
Wabash
Ohio
OHIO
White
Missouri
Kansas
Kanawha
James
Kentucky
New
Neosho
Roanoke
Cumberland
Ohio
St. Francis
Yadkin
White
Mississippi
TENNESSEE
Broad
Pee Dee
Arkansas
Tennessee
Santee
Ouachita
LOWER MISSISSIPPI
ATLANTIC OCEAN
Coosa
Ocmulgee
Savannah
Yazoo
SOUTH ATLANTIC
Tombigbee
Altamaha
Red
Black
Alabama
Chattahoochee
Sabine
Pearl
Flint
Trinity
Mobile
Apalachicola
St. Johns
Mississippi
Lake Okeechobee
Gulf of Mexico
Rivers
Drainage Basin Boundary
0 100 200 300 400 500 mi
0 100 200 300 400 500 km
© GeoSystems Global Corp.

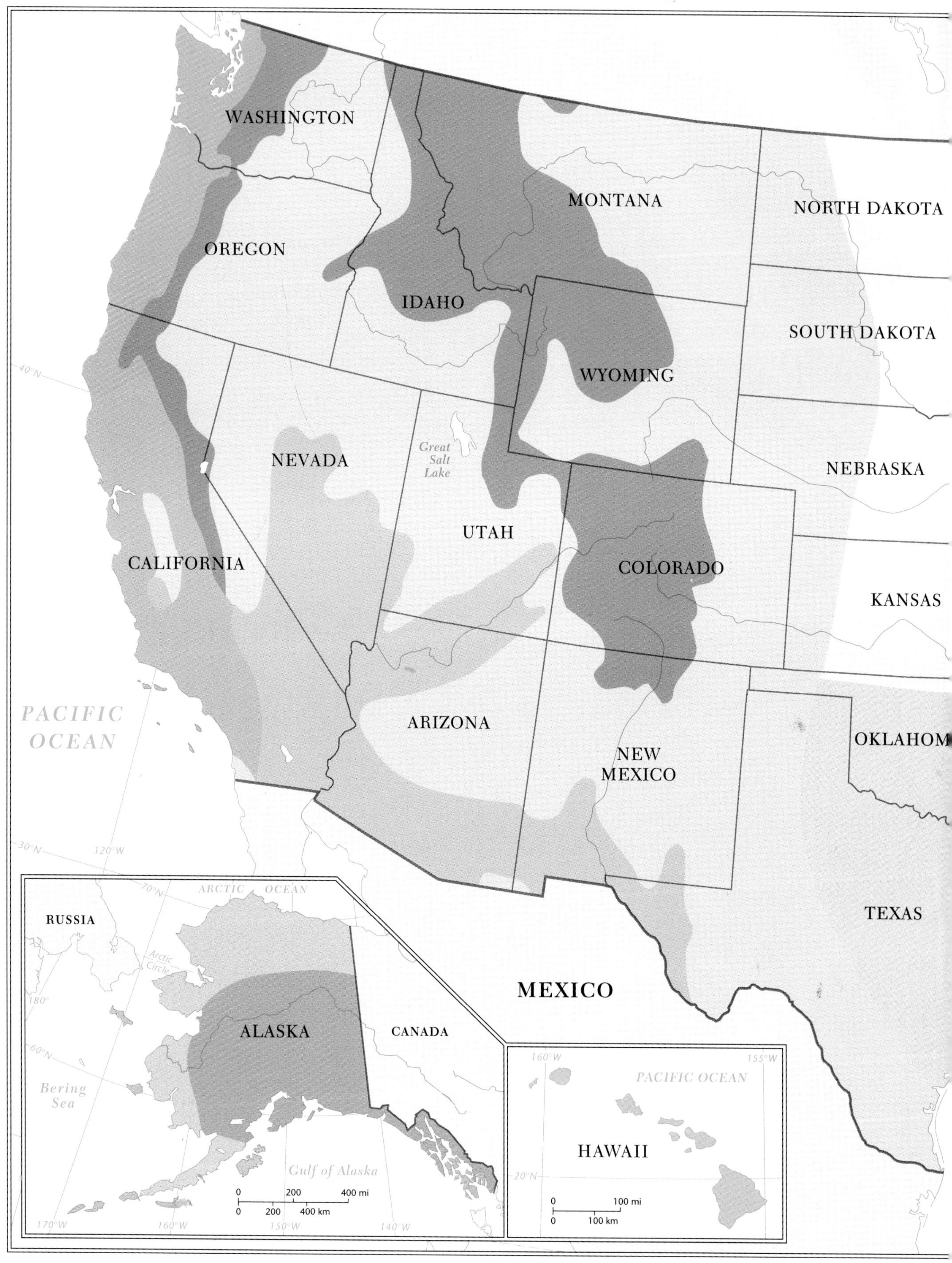
WASHINGTON
OREGON
IDAHO
MONTANA
NORTH DAKOTA
SOUTH DAKOTA
WYOMING
NEBRASKA
NEVADA
Great Salt Lake
UTAH
CALIFORNIA
COLORADO
KANSAS
PACIFIC OCEAN
ARIZONA
NEW MEXICO
OKLAHOM
TEXAS
MEXICO
40°N
30°N
120°W
RUSSIA
ARCTIC OCEAN
Arctic Circle
70°N
180°
ALASKA
CANADA
60°N
Bering Sea
Gulf of Alaska
0 200 400 mi
0 200 400 km
170°W
160°W
150°W
140°W
160°W
155°W
PACIFIC OCEAN
HAWAII
20°N
0 100 mi
0 100 km

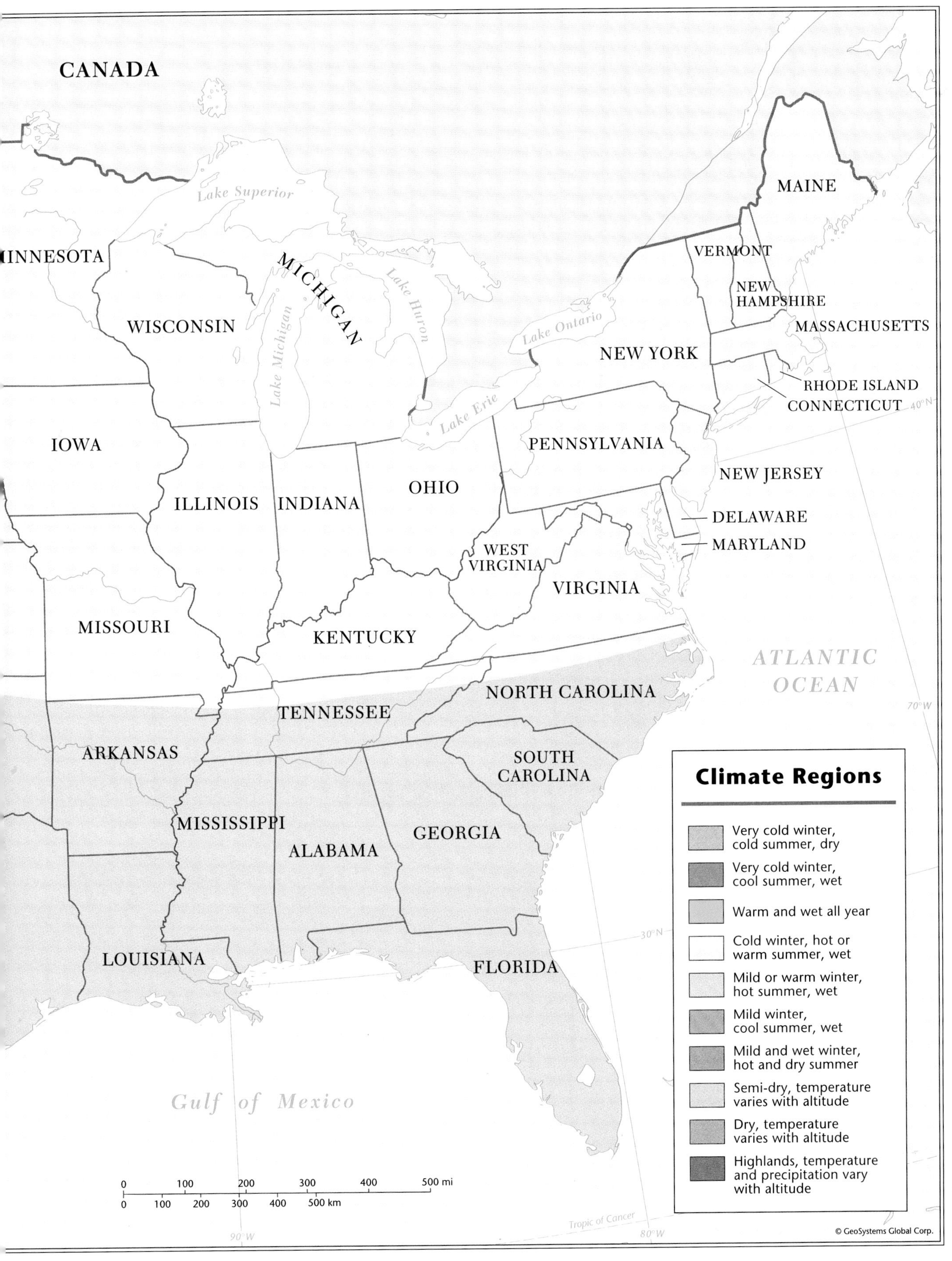
CANADA
MINNESOTA
WISCONSIN
MICHIGAN
Lake Superior
Lake Michigan
Lake Huron
Lake Ontario
Lake Erie
MAINE
VERMONT
NEW HAMPSHIRE
MASSACHUSETTS
NEW YORK
RHODE ISLAND
CONNECTICUT
IOWA
ILLINOIS
INDIANA
OHIO
PENNSYLVANIA
NEW JERSEY
DELAWARE
MARYLAND
WEST VIRGINIA
VIRGINIA
MISSOURI
KENTUCKY
ATLANTIC OCEAN
NORTH CAROLINA
TENNESSEE
ARKANSAS
SOUTH CAROLINA
MISSISSIPPI
ALABAMA
GEORGIA
LOUISIANA
FLORIDA
Gulf of Mexico
40° N
30° N
70° W
80° W
90° W
Tropic of Cancer
0 100 200 300 400 500 mi
0 100 200 300 400 500 km
Climate Regions
Very cold winter, cold summer, dry
Very cold winter, cool summer, wet
Warm and wet all year
Cold winter, hot or warm summer, wet
Mild or warm winter, hot summer, wet
Mild winter, cool summer, wet
Mild and wet winter, hot and dry summer
Semi-dry, temperature varies with altitude
Dry, temperature varies with altitude
Highlands, temperature and precipitation vary with altitude
© GeoSystems Global Corp.

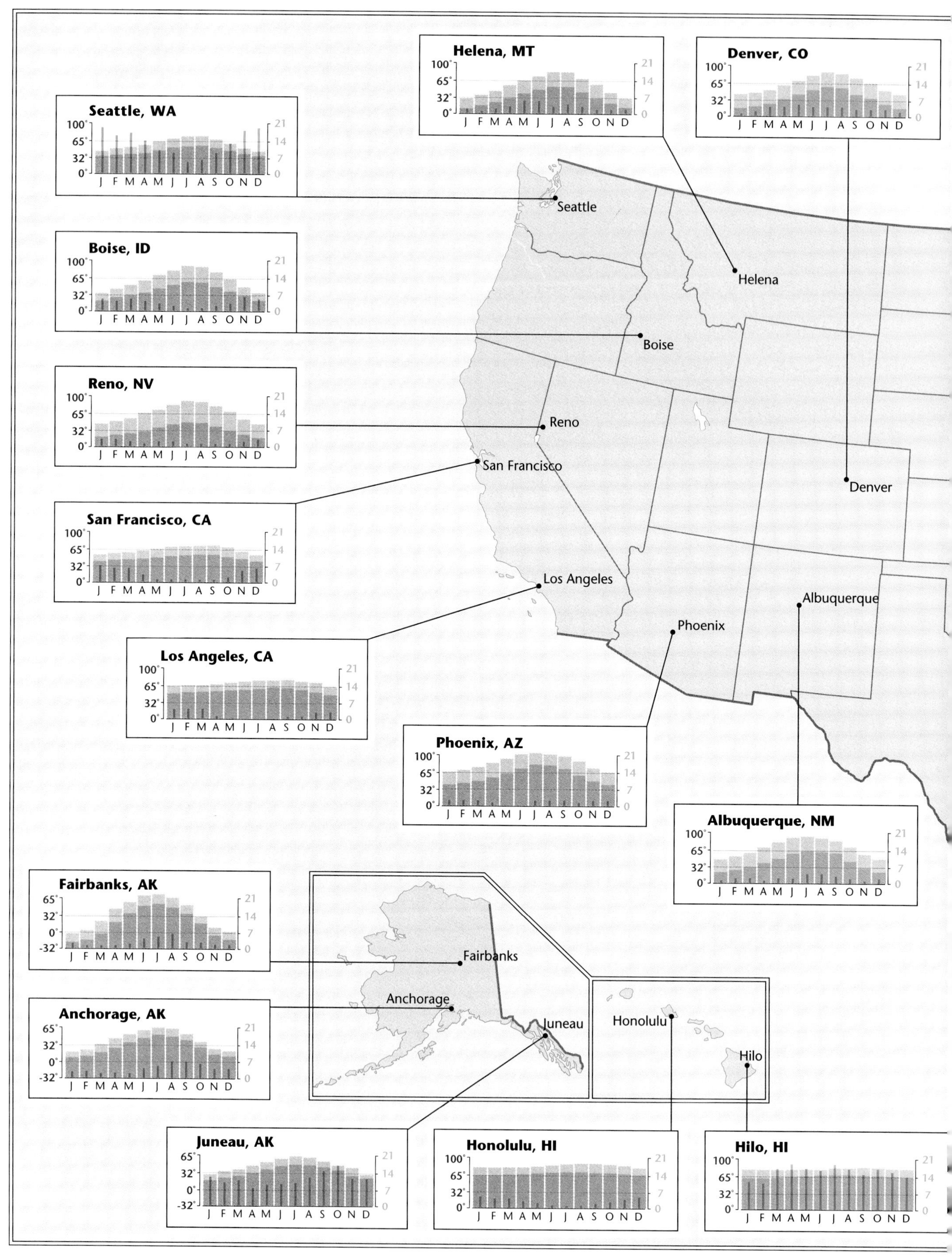
Helena, MT
Denver, CO
Seattle, WA
Boise, ID
Reno, NV
San Francisco, CA
Los Angeles, CA
Phoenix, AZ
Albuquerque, NM
Fairbanks, AK
Anchorage, AK
Juneau, AK
Honolulu, HI
Hilo, HI
100°
65°
32°
0°
-32°
21
14
7
0
J F M A M J J A S O N D
Seattle
Helena
Boise
Reno
San Francisco
Denver
Los Angeles
Albuquerque
Phoenix
Fairbanks
Anchorage
Juneau
Honolulu
Hilo

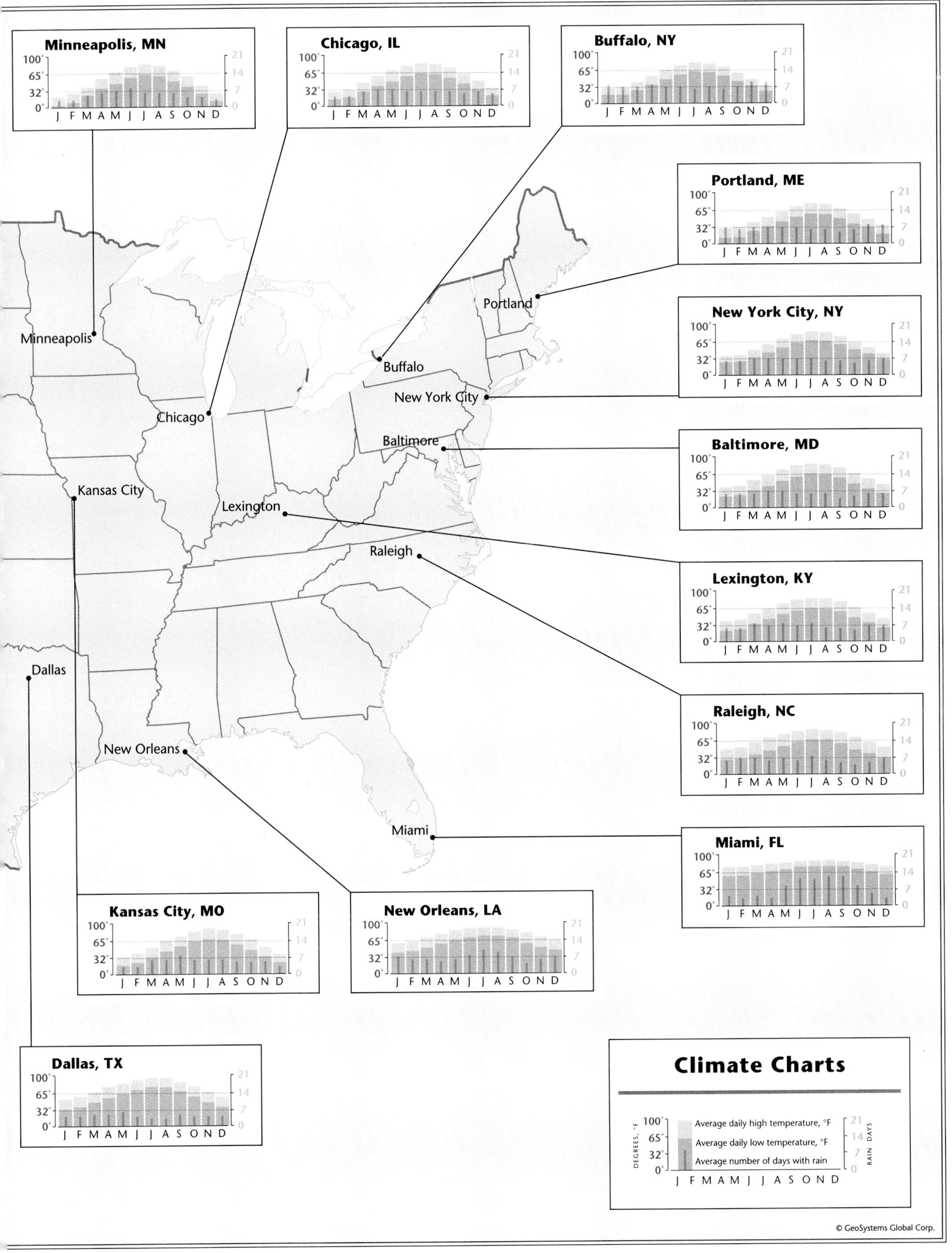
Minneapolis, MN
Chicago, IL
Buffalo, NY
Portland, ME
New York City, NY
Baltimore, MD
Lexington, KY
Raleigh, NC
Miami, FL
Kansas City, MO
New Orleans, LA
Dallas, TX
100°
65°
32°
0°
21
14
7
0
J F M A M J J A S O N D
Minneapolis
Chicago
Buffalo
Portland
New York City
Baltimore
Kansas City
Lexington
Raleigh
Dallas
New Orleans
Miami
Climate Charts
DEGREES, °F
Average daily high temperature, °F
Average daily low temperature, °F
Average number of days with rain
RAIN DAYS

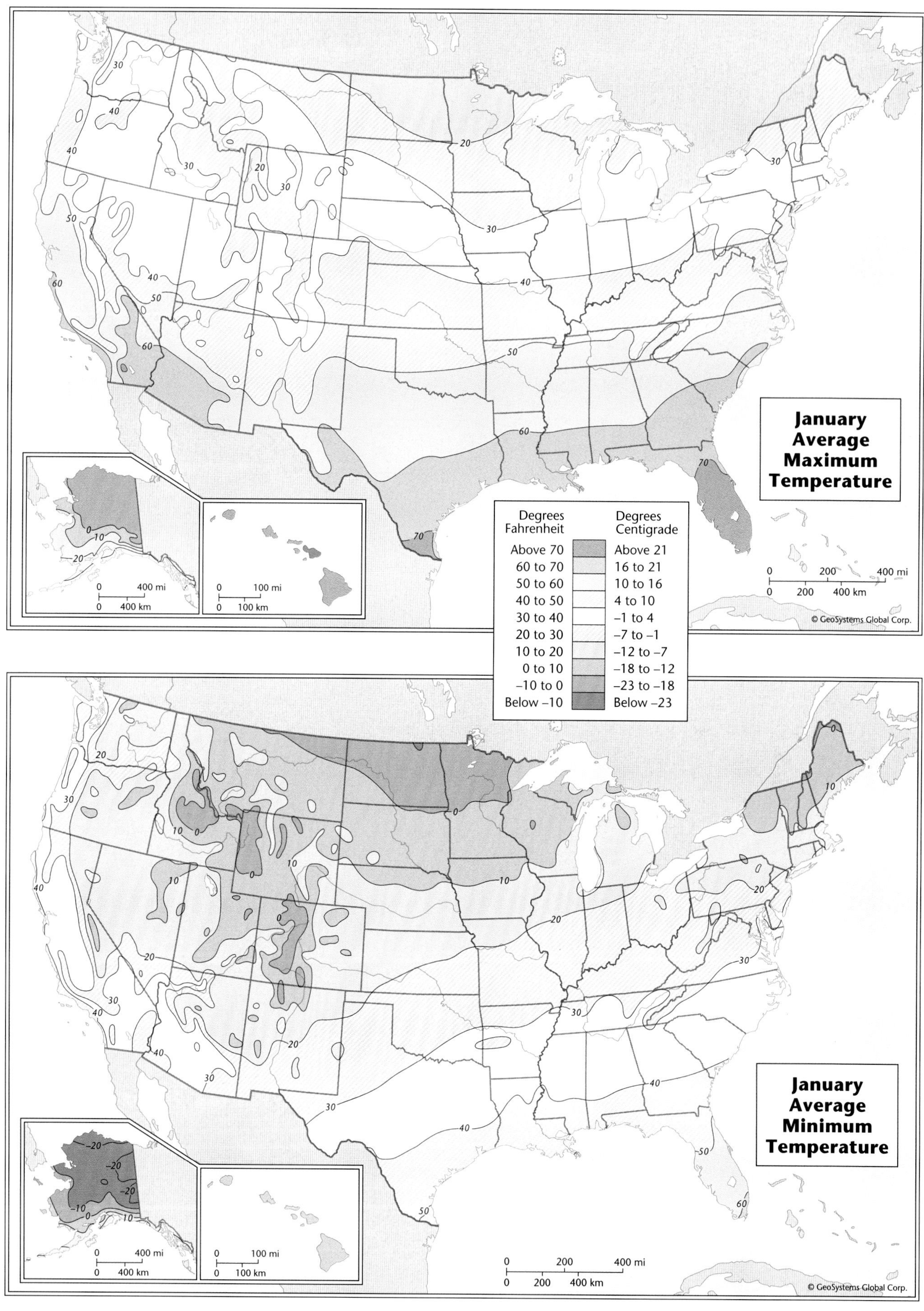
January Average Maximum Temperature
Degrees Fahrenheit
Degrees Centigrade
Above 70
Above 21
60 to 70
16 to 21
50 to 60
10 to 16
40 to 50
4 to 10
30 to 40
–1 to 4
20 to 30
–7 to –1
10 to 20
–12 to –7
0 to 10
–18 to –12
–10 to 0
–23 to –18
Below –10
Below –23
0 200 400 mi
0 200 400 km
0 400 mi
0 400 km
0 100 mi
0 100 km
© GeoSystems Global Corp.
January Average Minimum Temperature
0 200 400 mi
0 200 400 km
© GeoSystems Global Corp.

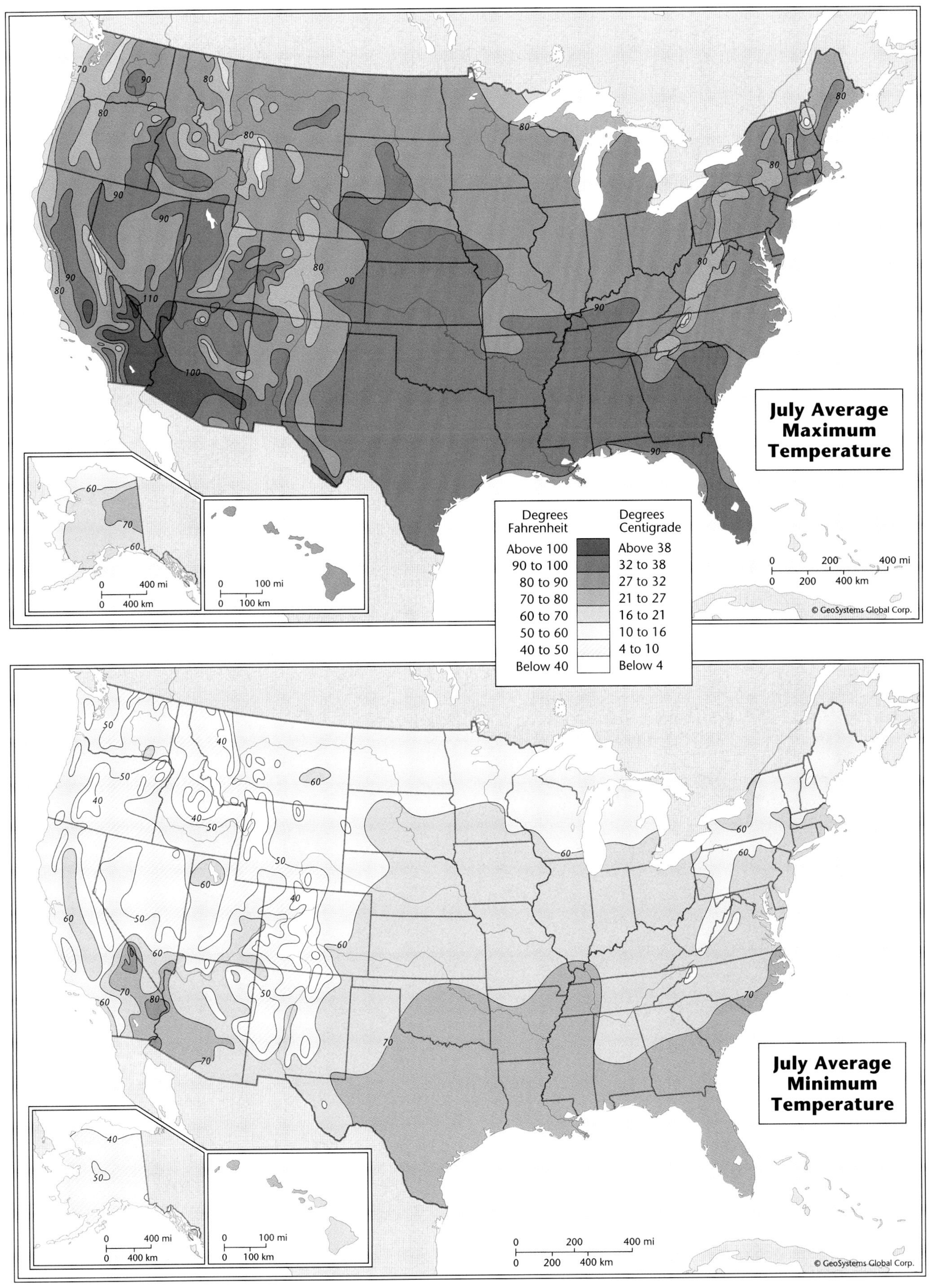
July Average Maximum Temperature
Degrees Fahrenheit
Degrees Centigrade
Above 100 | Above 38
90 to 100 | 32 to 38
80 to 90 | 27 to 32
70 to 80 | 21 to 27
60 to 70 | 16 to 21
50 to 60 | 10 to 16
40 to 50 | 4 to 10
Below 40 | Below 4
0 200 400 mi
0 200 400 km
0 400 mi
0 400 km
0 100 mi
0 100 km
© GeoSystems Global Corp.
July Average Minimum Temperature
© GeoSystems Global Corp.

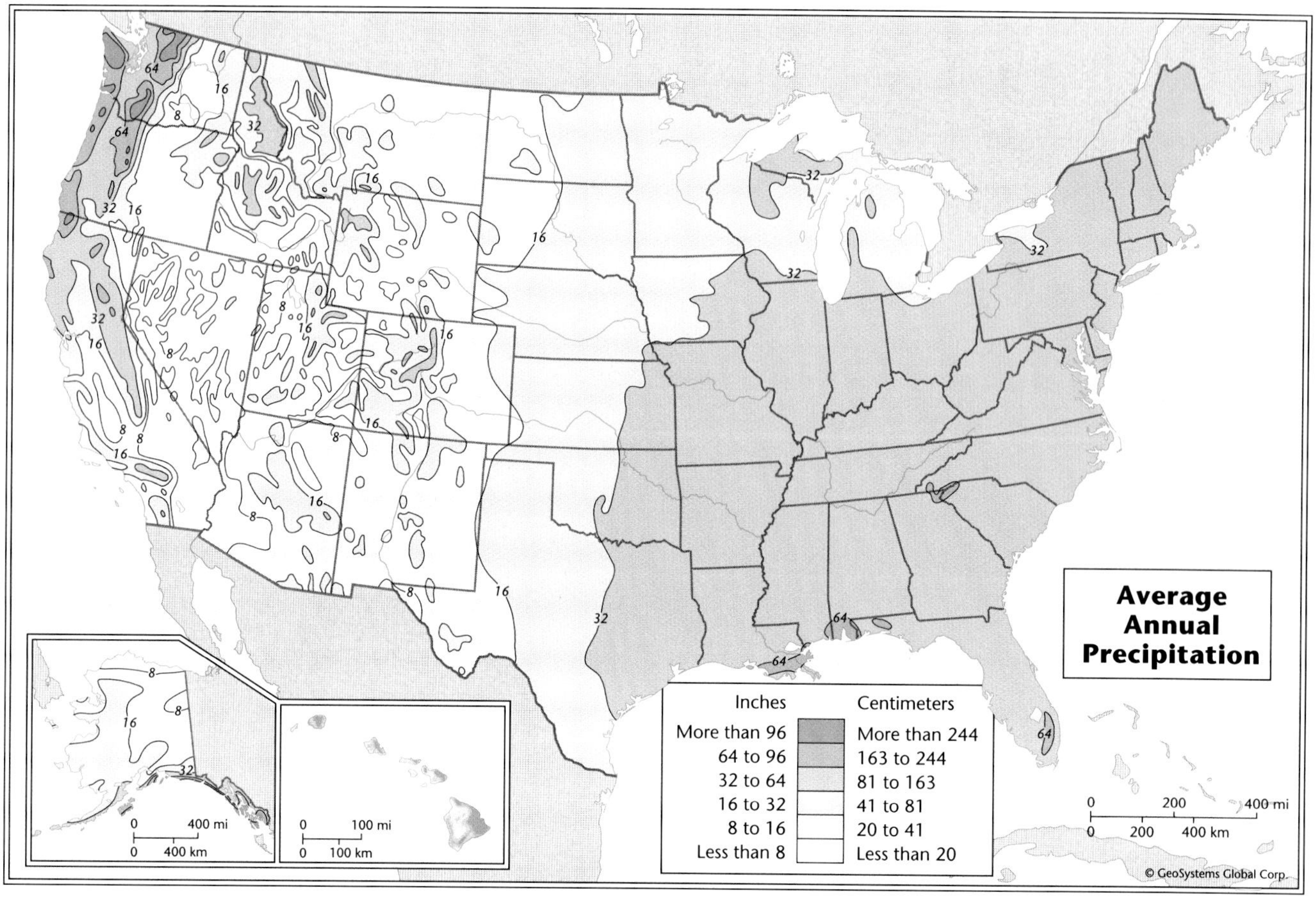

# Precipitation

## Average Annual Precipitation

| Inches | Centimeters |
|---|---|
| More than 96 | More than 244 |
| 64 to 96 | 163 to 244 |
| 32 to 64 | 81 to 163 |
| 16 to 32 | 41 to 81 |
| 8 to 16 | 20 to 41 |
| Less than 8 | Less than 20 |

0 200 400 mi
0 200 400 km

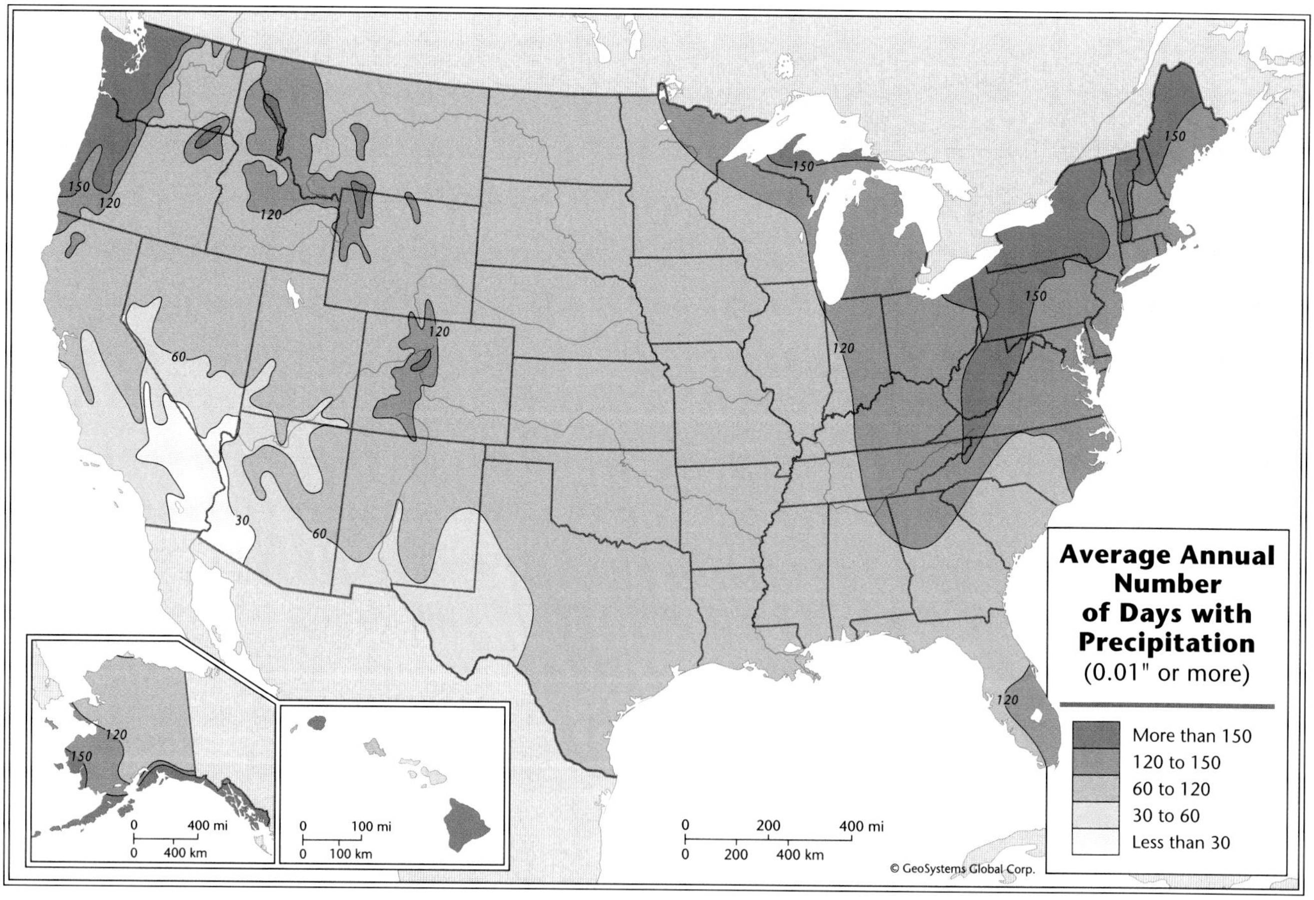

## Average Annual Number of Days with Precipitation (0.01" or more)

- More than 150
- 120 to 150
- 60 to 120
- 30 to 60
- Less than 30

0 200 400 mi
0 200 400 km

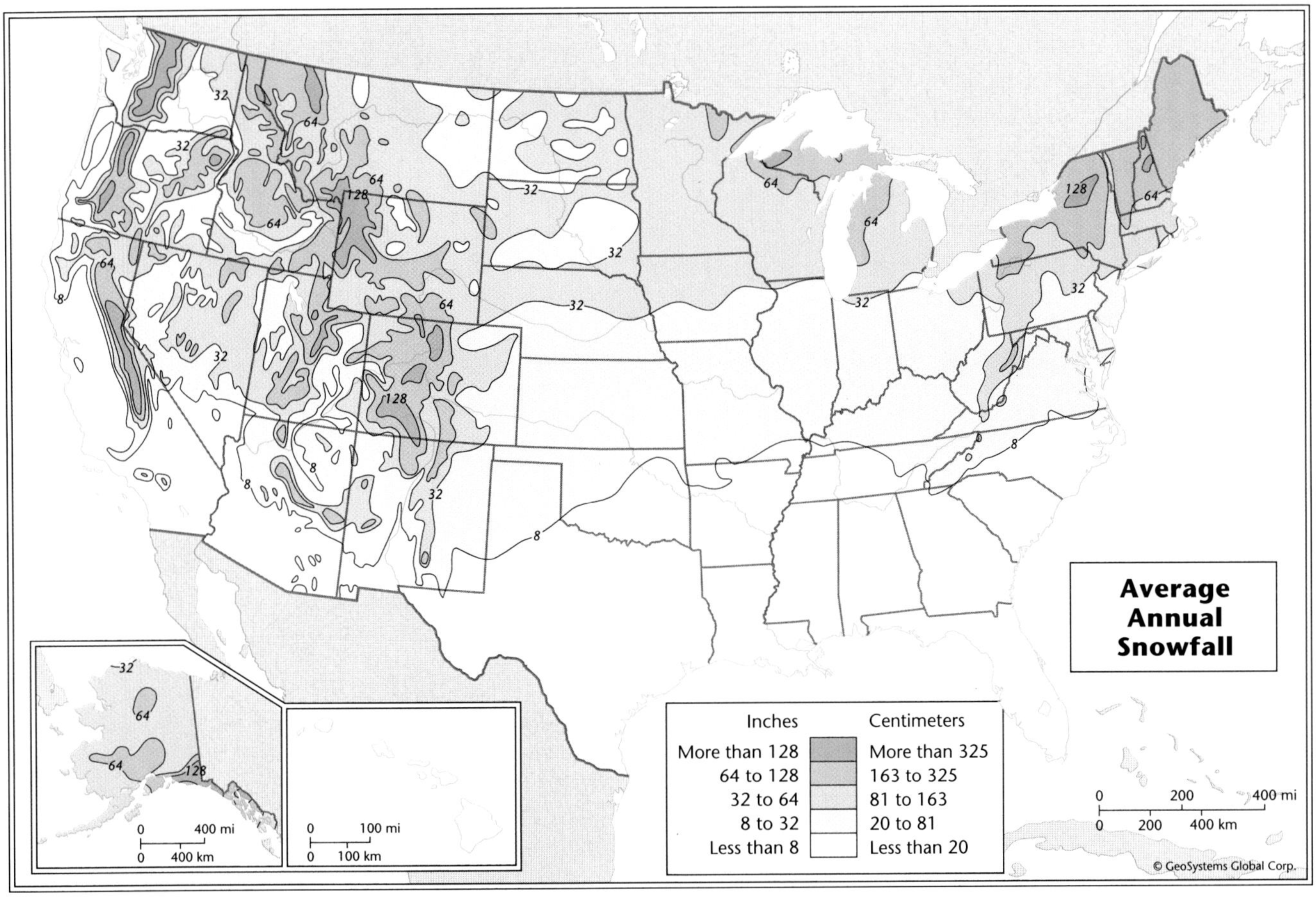
Average Annual Snowfall
Inches
Centimeters
More than 128
More than 325
64 to 128
163 to 325
32 to 64
81 to 163
8 to 32
20 to 81
Less than 8
Less than 20
32
64
128
8
0 200 400 mi
0 200 400 km
0 400 mi
0 400 km
0 100 mi
0 100 km
© GeoSystems Global Corp.

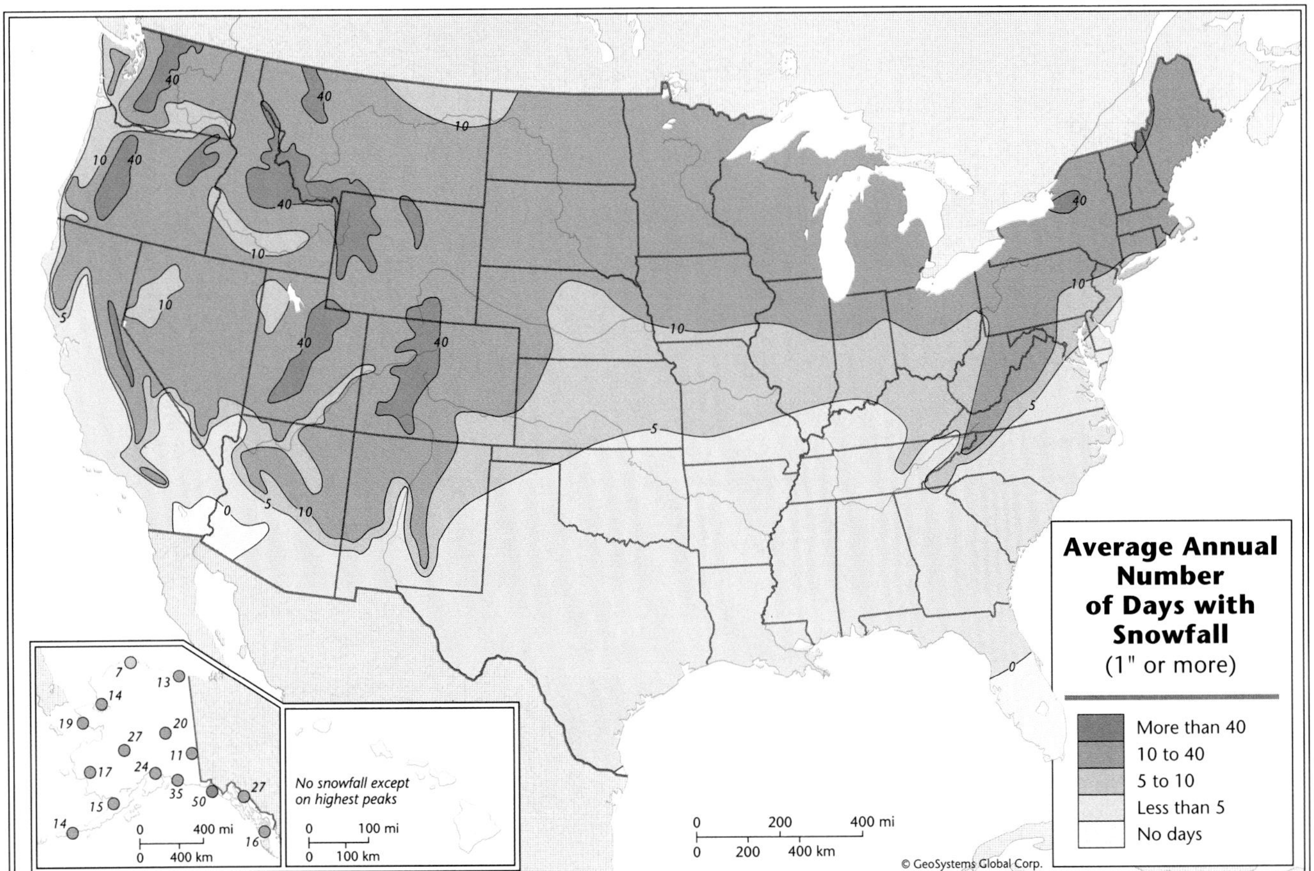
Average Annual Number of Days with Snowfall
(1" or more)
More than 40
10 to 40
5 to 10
Less than 5
No days
40
10
5
0
7
13
14
19
20
27
11
17
24
35
50
15
16
No snowfall except on highest peaks
0 400 mi
0 400 km
0 100 mi
0 100 km
0 200 400 mi
0 200 400 km
© GeoSystems Global Corp.

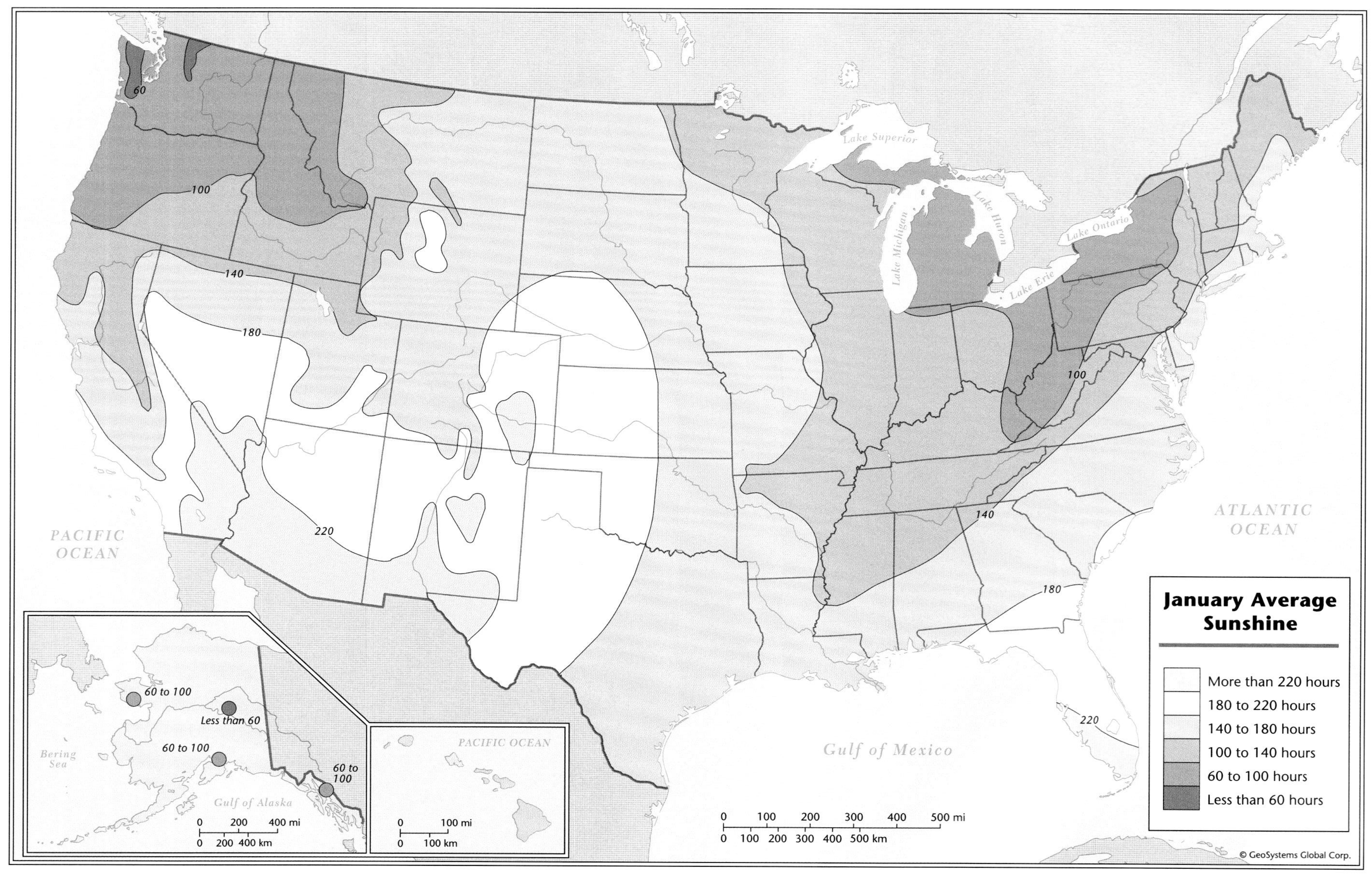
January Average Sunshine
More than 220 hours
180 to 220 hours
140 to 180 hours
100 to 140 hours
60 to 100 hours
Less than 60 hours
© GeoSystems Global Corp.
PACIFIC OCEAN
ATLANTIC OCEAN
Gulf of Mexico
Lake Superior
Lake Michigan
Lake Huron
Lake Erie
Lake Ontario
60
100
140
180
220
100
140
180
220
0 100 200 300 400 500 mi
0 100 200 300 400 500 km
60 to 100
Less than 60
60 to 100
60 to 100
Bering Sea
Gulf of Alaska
0 200 400 mi
0 200 400 km
PACIFIC OCEAN
0 100 mi
0 100 km

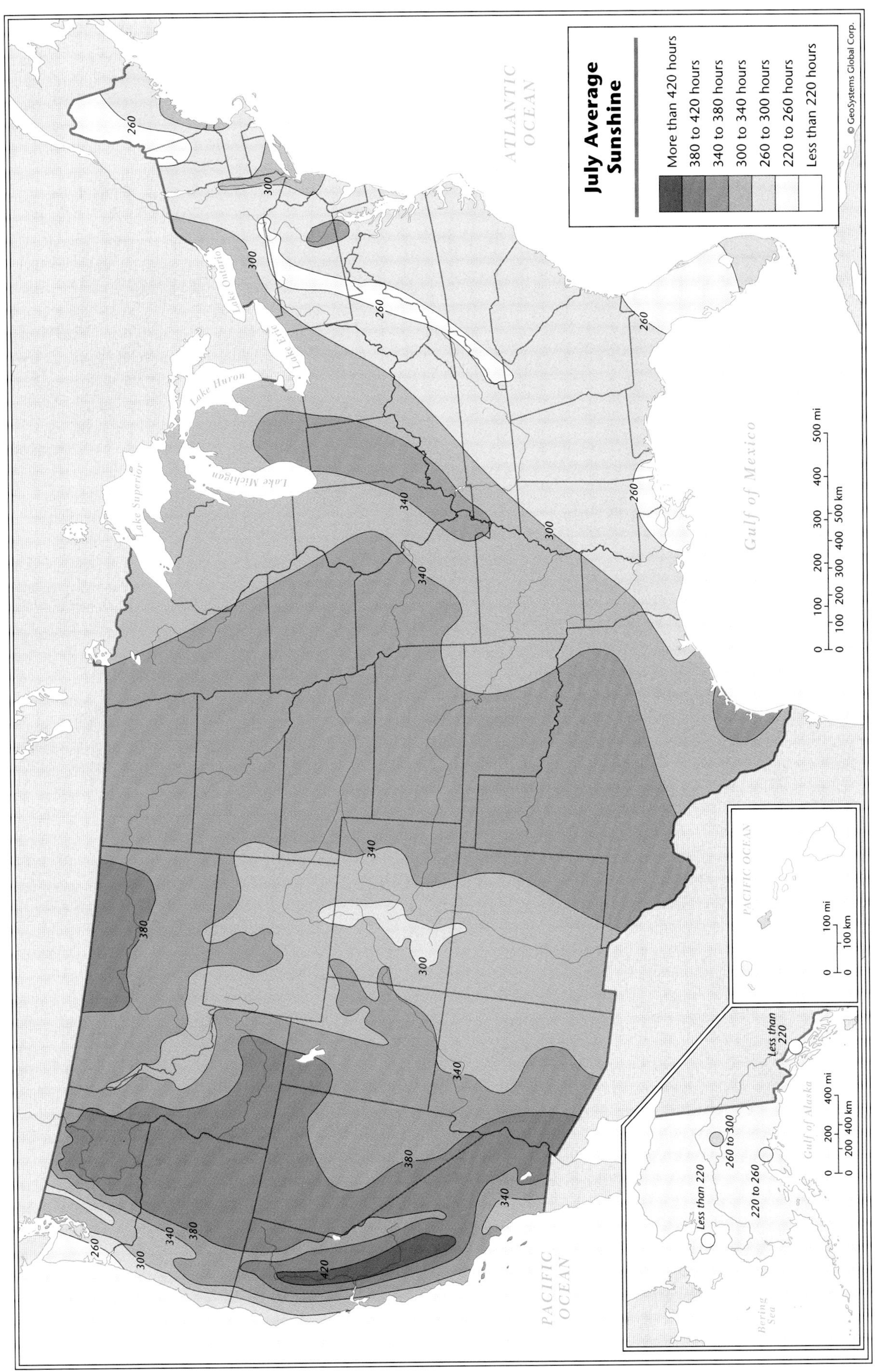

July Average Sunshine
More than 420 hours
380 to 420 hours
340 to 380 hours
300 to 340 hours
260 to 300 hours
220 to 260 hours
Less than 220 hours
© GeoSystems Global Corp.
ATLANTIC OCEAN
PACIFIC OCEAN
Gulf of Mexico
Lake Superior
Lake Michigan
Lake Huron
Lake Erie
Lake Ontario
Gulf of Alaska
Bering Sea
Less than 220
260 to 300
220 to 260
0 100 200 300 400 500 mi
0 100 200 300 400 500 km
0 200 400 mi
0 200 400 km
0 100 mi
0 100 km
420
380
340
300
260

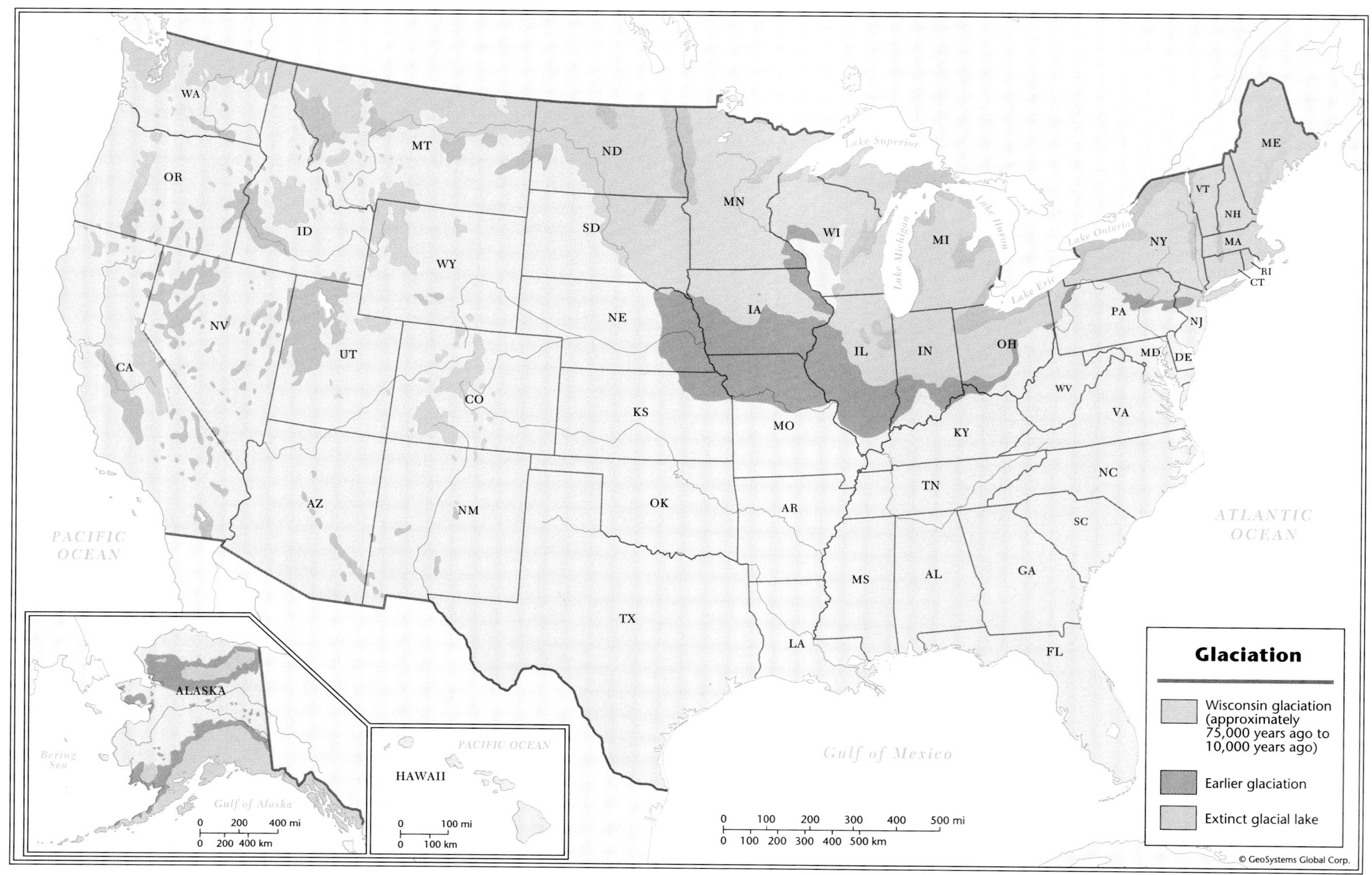
Glaciation
Wisconsin glaciation (approximately 75,000 years ago to 10,000 years ago)
Earlier glaciation
Extinct glacial lake
© GeoSystems Global Corp.
PACIFIC OCEAN
ATLANTIC OCEAN
Gulf of Mexico
Lake Superior
Lake Michigan
Lake Huron
Lake Erie
Lake Ontario
WA
OR
CA
ID
NV
MT
WY
UT
AZ
CO
NM
ND
SD
NE
KS
OK
TX
MN
IA
MO
AR
LA
WI
IL
MI
IN
OH
KY
TN
MS
AL
GA
FL
SC
NC
VA
WV
MD
DE
PA
NJ
NY
VT
NH
MA
RI
CT
ME
ALASKA
Bering Sea
Gulf of Alaska
0 200 400 mi
0 200 400 km
HAWAII
PACIFIC OCEAN
0 100 mi
0 100 km
0 100 200 300 400 500 mi
0 100 200 300 400 500 km

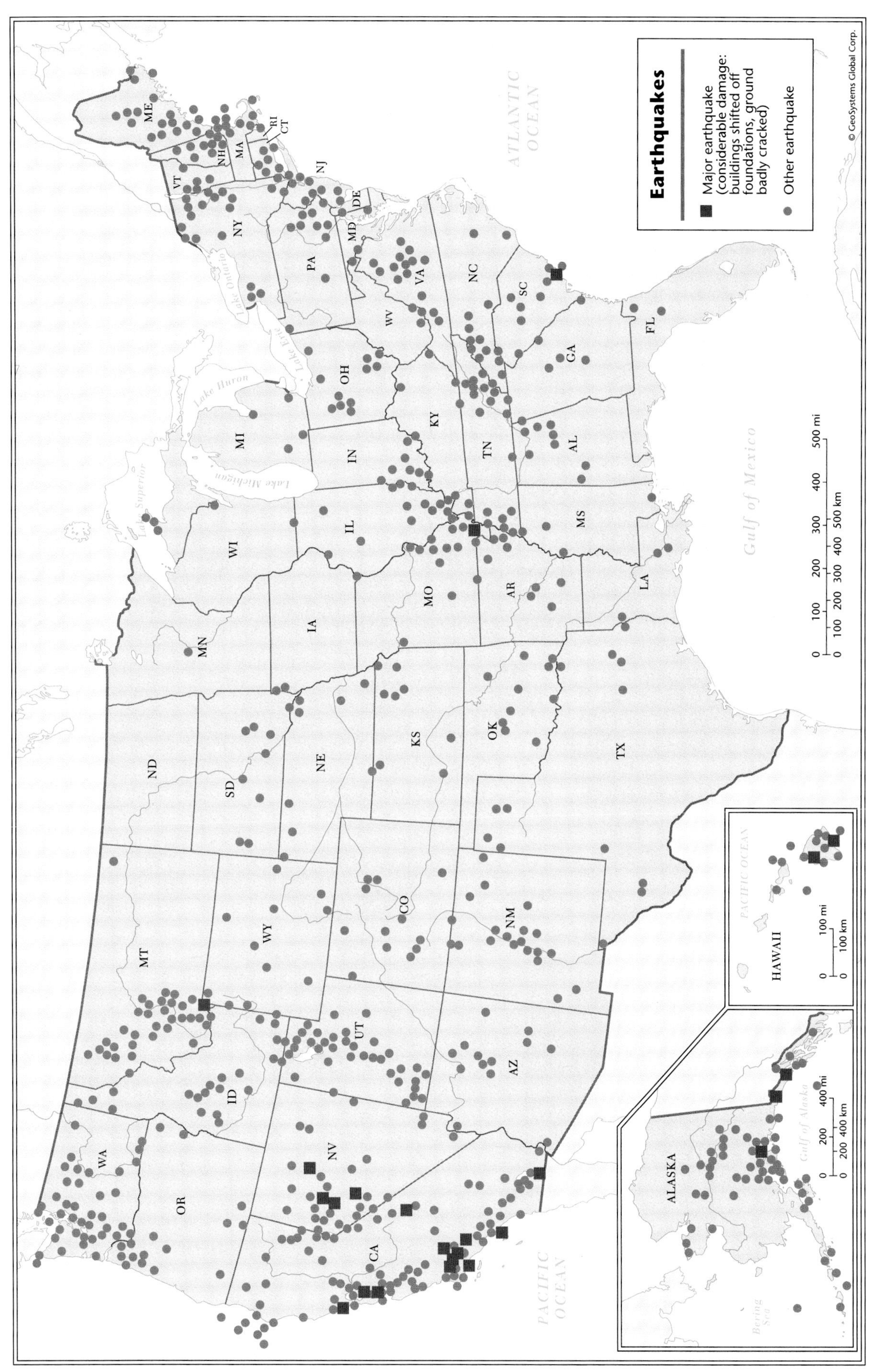
Earthquakes
Major earthquake (considerable damage: buildings shifted off foundations, ground badly cracked)
Other earthquake
© GeoSystems Global Corp.
ATLANTIC OCEAN
PACIFIC OCEAN
Gulf of Mexico
Lake Superior
Lake Michigan
Lake Huron
Lake Erie
Lake Ontario
ME
NH
VT
MA
RI
CT
NY
NJ
PA
DE
MD
VA
WV
NC
SC
GA
FL
AL
MS
TN
KY
OH
IN
MI
IL
WI
MN
IA
MO
AR
LA
TX
OK
KS
NE
SD
ND
MT
WY
CO
NM
AZ
UT
ID
NV
CA
OR
WA
0 100 200 300 400 500 mi
0 100 200 300 400 500 km
HAWAII
PACIFIC OCEAN
0 100 mi
0 100 km
ALASKA
Gulf of Alaska
Bering Sea
0 200 400 mi
0 200 400 km

WASHINGTON
OREGON
IDAHO
MONTANA
NORTH DAKOTA
SOUTH DAKOTA
WYOMING
NEBRASKA
NEVADA
Great Salt Lake
UTAH
CALIFORNIA
COLORADO
KANSAS
PACIFIC OCEAN
ARIZONA
NEW MEXICO
OKLAHO
TEXAS
MEXICO
40°N
30°N
120°W
RUSSIA
ARCTIC OCEAN
70°N
Arctic Circle
180°
ALASKA
CANADA
60°N
Bering Sea
Gulf of Alaska
0 200 400 mi
0 200 400 km
170°W
160°W
150°W
140°W
160°W
155°W
PACIFIC OCEAN
HAWAII
20°N
0 100 mi
0 100 km

CANADA
Lake Superior
MINNESOTA
MICHIGAN
Lake Huron
Lake Michigan
Lake Ontario
Lake Erie
WISCONSIN
MAINE
VERMONT
NEW HAMPSHIRE
MASSACHUSETTS
NEW YORK
RHODE ISLAND
CONNECTICUT
IOWA
PENNSYLVANIA
NEW JERSEY
ILLINOIS
INDIANA
OHIO
DELAWARE
MARYLAND
WEST VIRGINIA
VIRGINIA
MISSOURI
KENTUCKY
ATLANTIC OCEAN
NORTH CAROLINA
TENNESSEE
ARKANSAS
SOUTH CAROLINA
MISSISSIPPI
ALABAMA
GEORGIA
LOUISIANA
FLORIDA
Gulf of Mexico
40°N
30°N
70°W
80°W
90°W
Tropic of Cancer
0 100 200 300 400 500 mi
0 100 200 300 400 500 km
Natural Vegetation
Tundra
Coniferous Forest
Deciduous Forest
Broadleaf Evergreen Forest
Tropical Rain Forest
Mixed Forest
Midlatitude Scrubland
Midlatitude Grassland
Desert
© GeoSystems Global Corp.

## Land Use

Seattle-Tacoma
WASHINGTON
Portland
OREGON
IDAHO
MONTANA
NORTH DAKOTA
SOUTH DAKOTA
WYOMING
NEBRASKA
Great Salt Lake
Salt Lake City
NEVADA
Sacramento
San Francisco-Oakland-San Jose
CALIFORNIA
UTAH
Denver
COLORADO
KANSAS
Las Vegas
Los Angeles
San Diego
PACIFIC OCEAN
ARIZONA
Phoenix
Tucson
Albuquerque
NEW MEXICO
OKLAHOM
Oklahoma City
Dallas-Fort Worth
El Paso
TEXAS
Austin
San Antonio
MEXICO
RUSSIA
ARCTIC OCEAN
ALASKA
CANADA
Bering Sea
Gulf of Alaska
0 200 400 mi
0 200 400 km
PACIFIC OCEAN
Honolulu
HAWAII
0 100 mi
0 100 km

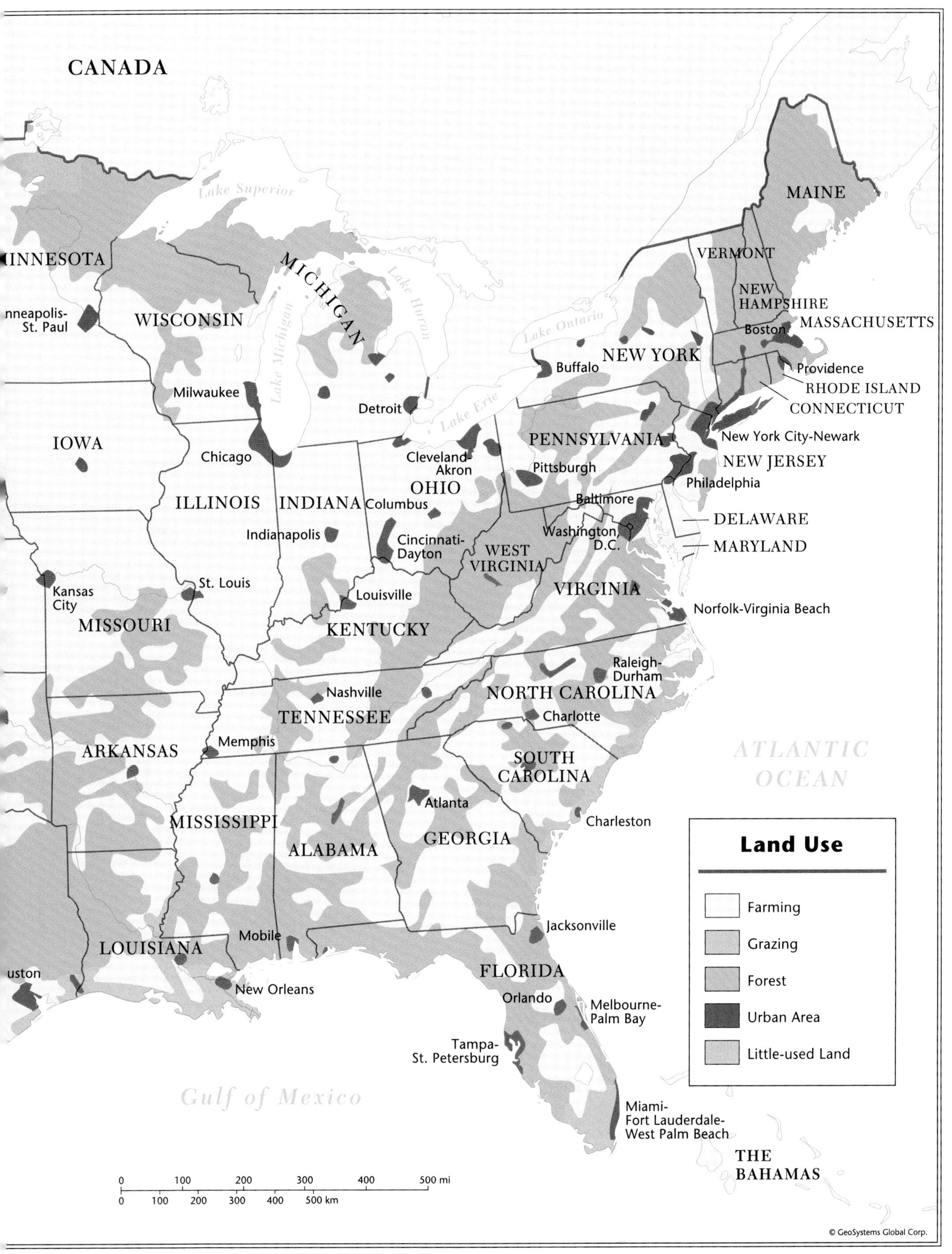

CANADA
Lake Superior
MINNESOTA
Minneapolis-St. Paul
WISCONSIN
MICHIGAN
Lake Michigan
Lake Huron
Lake Ontario
Lake Erie
Milwaukee
Detroit
IOWA
Chicago
Cleveland-Akron
Buffalo
NEW YORK
MAINE
VERMONT
NEW HAMPSHIRE
MASSACHUSETTS
Boston
Providence
RHODE ISLAND
CONNECTICUT
New York City-Newark
NEW JERSEY
PENNSYLVANIA
Pittsburgh
Philadelphia
OHIO
ILLINOIS
INDIANA
Columbus
Baltimore
DELAWARE
MARYLAND
Washington, D.C.
Indianapolis
Cincinnati-Dayton
WEST VIRGINIA
Kansas City
St. Louis
Louisville
VIRGINIA
Norfolk-Virginia Beach
MISSOURI
KENTUCKY
Raleigh-Durham
NORTH CAROLINA
Nashville
TENNESSEE
Charlotte
Memphis
ARKANSAS
SOUTH CAROLINA
ATLANTIC OCEAN
Atlanta
MISSISSIPPI
Charleston
ALABAMA
GEORGIA
Land Use
Farming
Grazing
Forest
Urban Area
Little-used Land
Jacksonville
Mobile
LOUISIANA
Houston
New Orleans
FLORIDA
Orlando
Melbourne-Palm Bay
Tampa-St. Petersburg
Gulf of Mexico
Miami-Fort Lauderdale-West Palm Beach
THE BAHAMAS
0 100 200 300 400 500 mi
0 100 200 300 400 500 km
© GeoSystems Global Corp.

# Coal, Oil, and Natural Gas

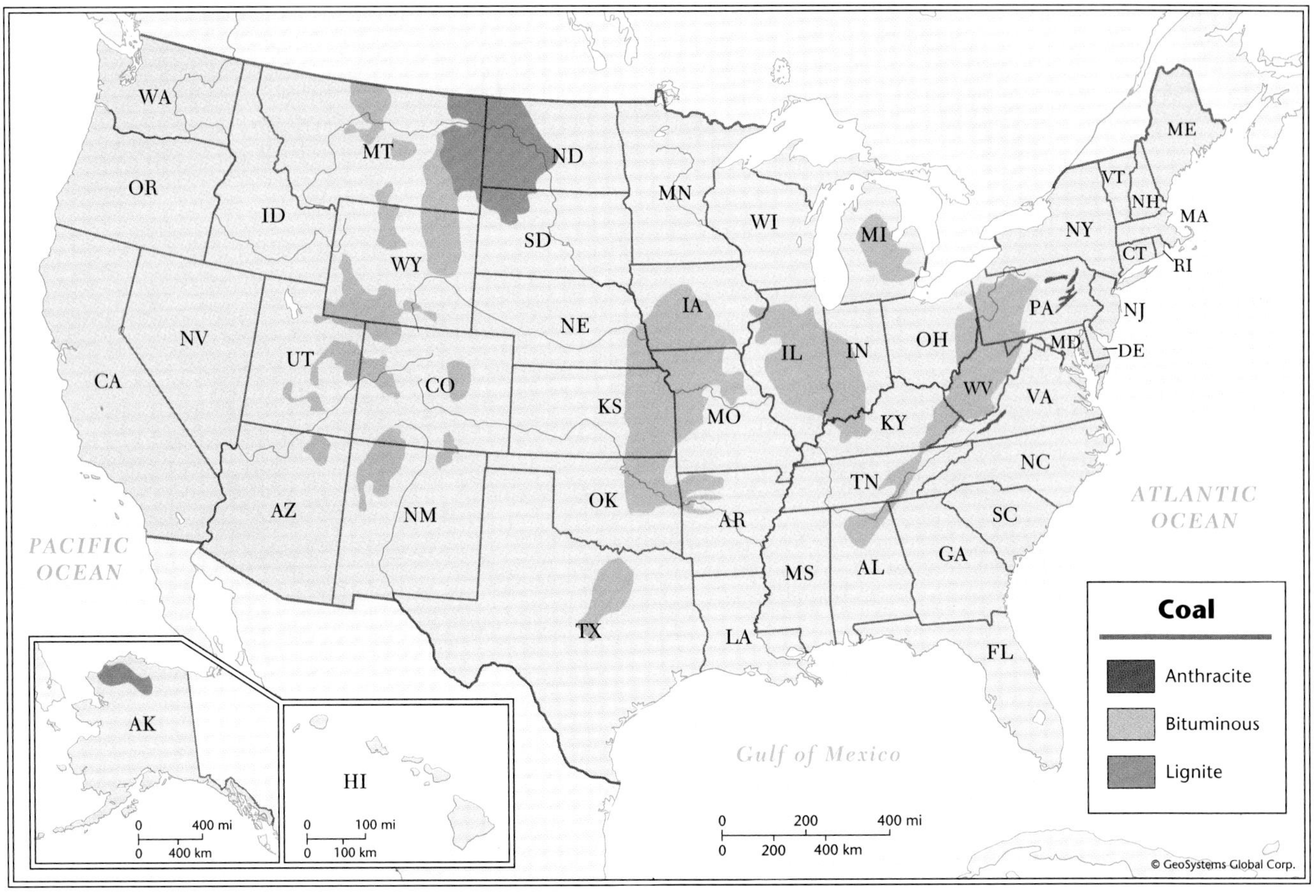

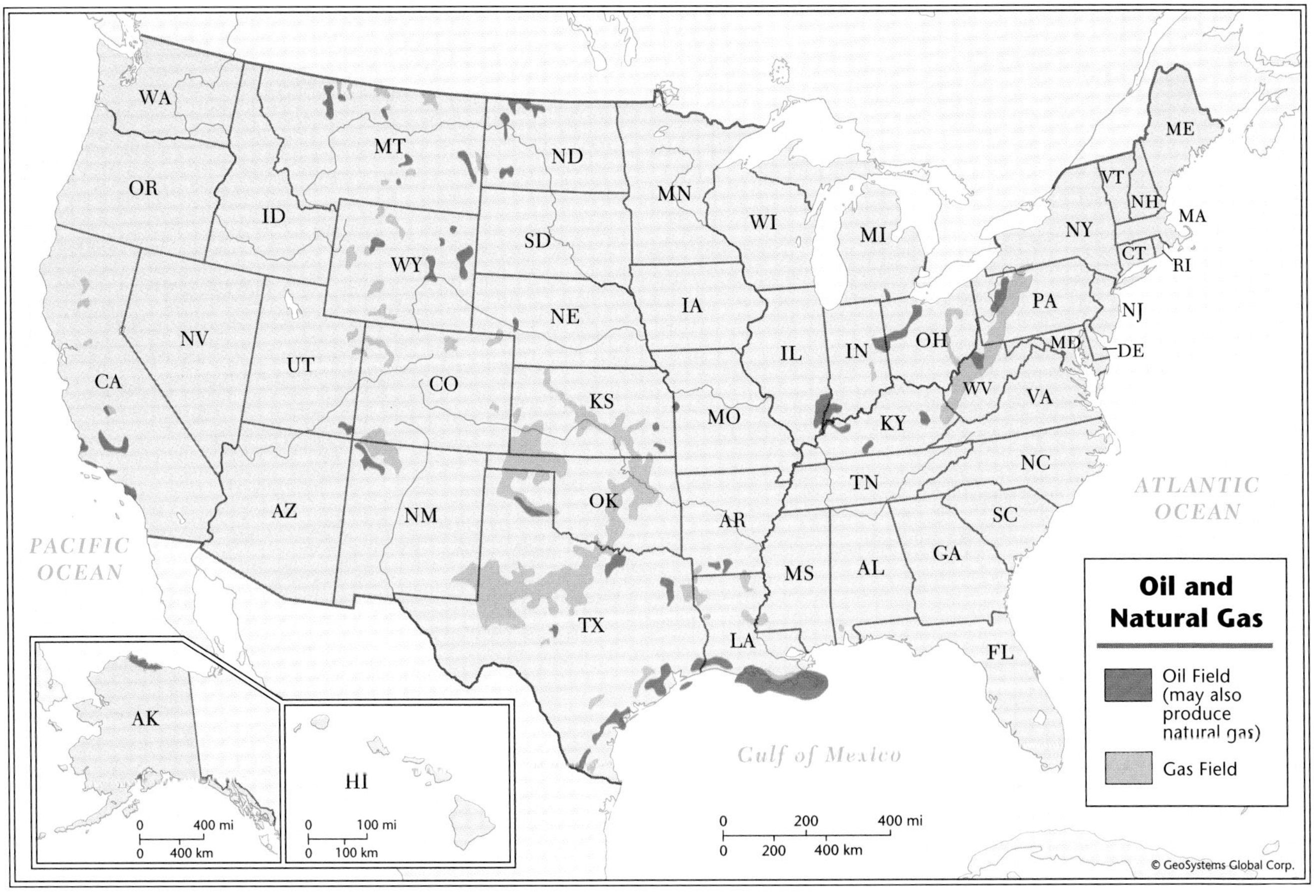

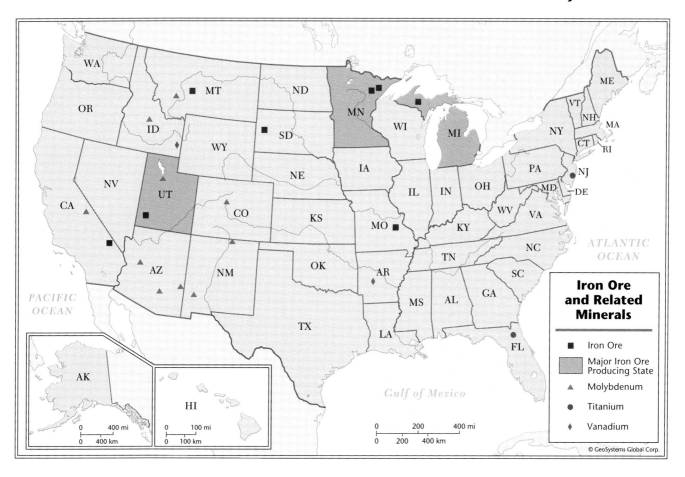

## Iron Ore and Related Minerals

- ■ Iron Ore
- Major Iron Ore Producing State
- ▲ Molybdenum
- ● Titanium
- ♦ Vanadium

PACIFIC OCEAN

ATLANTIC OCEAN

Gulf of Mexico

0 200 400 mi
0 200 400 km



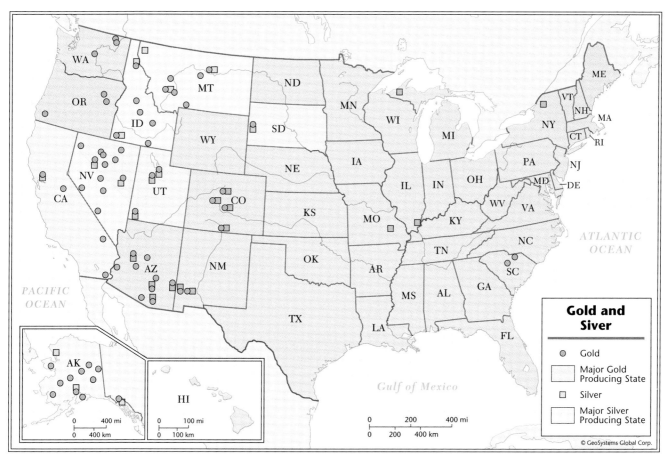

## Gold and Siver

- ● Gold
- Major Gold Producing State
- □ Silver
- Major Silver Producing State

PACIFIC OCEAN

ATLANTIC OCEAN

Gulf of Mexico

0 200 400 mi
0 200 400 km

# Major Minerals

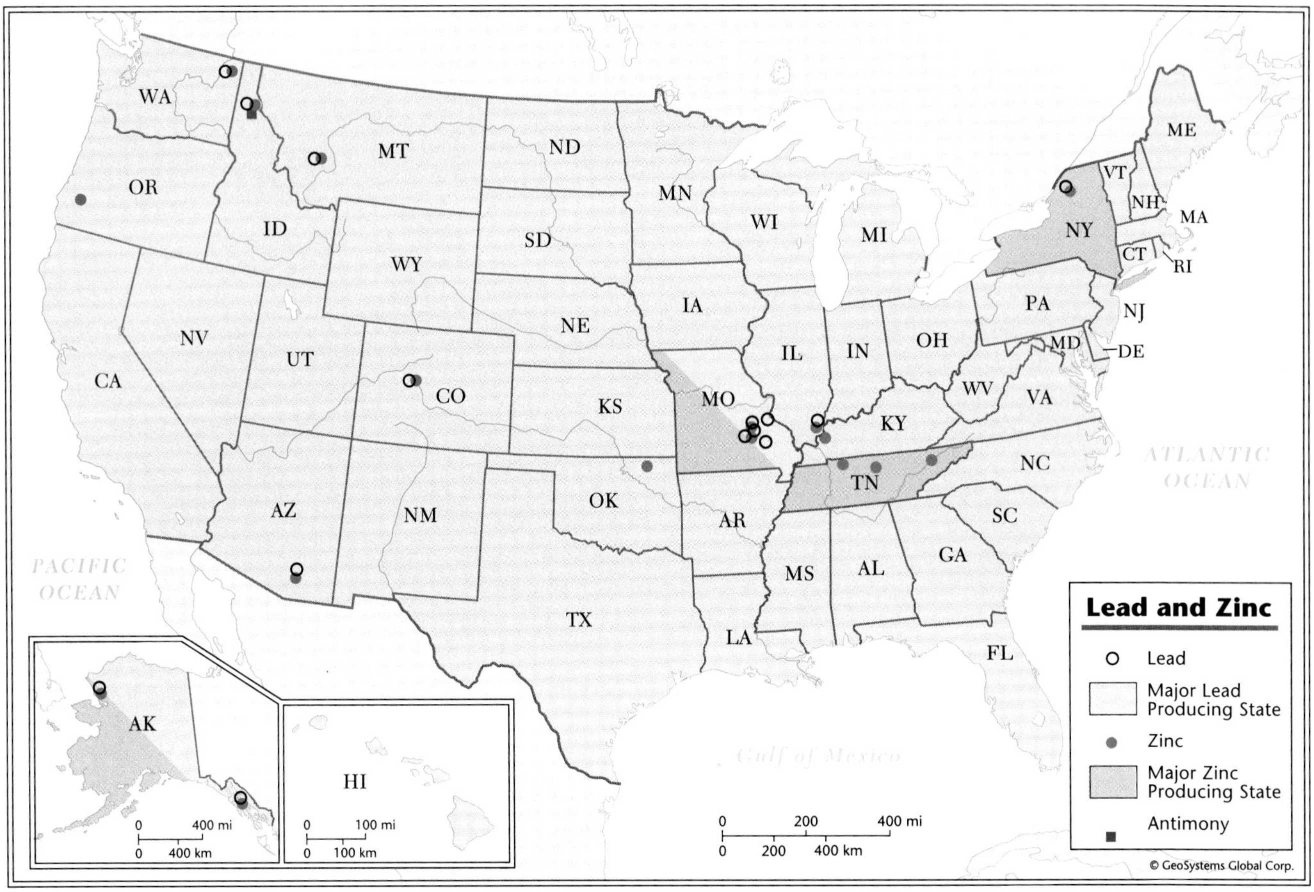

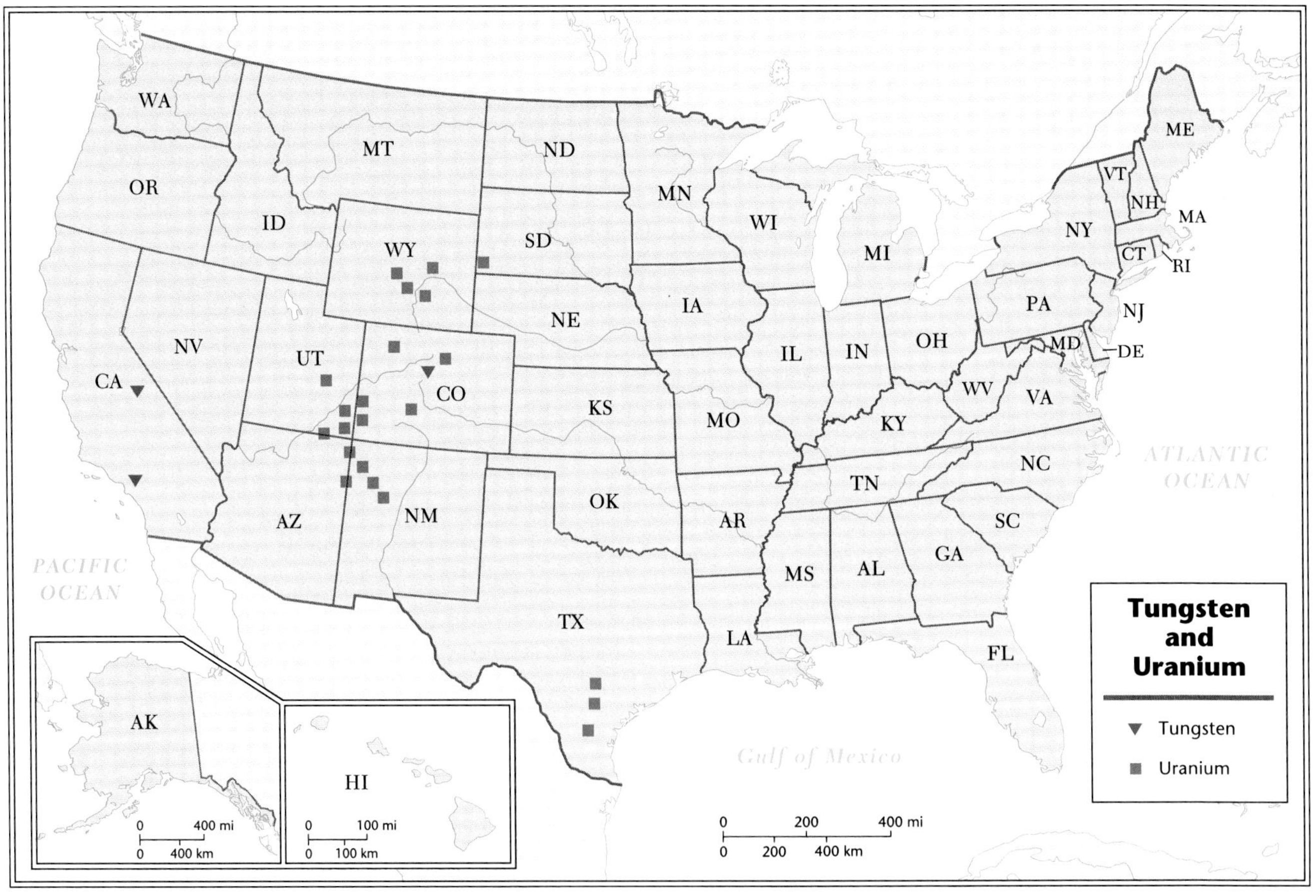

WA OR CA NV ID MT WY UT CO AZ NM ND SD NE KS OK TX MN IA MO AR LA WI IL MI IN OH KY TN MS AL GA FL SC NC VA WV MD DE PA NJ NY CT RI MA VT NH ME AK HI

PACIFIC OCEAN

ATLANTIC OCEAN

Gulf of Mexico

0 400 mi
0 400 km

0 100 mi
0 100 km

0 200 400 mi
0 200 400 km

**Lead and Zinc**

- Lead
- Major Lead Producing State
- Zinc
- Major Zinc Producing State
- Antimony



WA OR CA NV ID MT WY UT CO AZ NM ND SD NE KS OK TX MN IA MO AR LA WI IL MI IN OH KY TN MS AL GA FL SC NC VA WV MD DE PA NJ NY CT RI MA VT NH ME AK HI

PACIFIC OCEAN

ATLANTIC OCEAN

Gulf of Mexico

0 400 mi
0 400 km

0 100 mi
0 100 km

0 200 400 mi
0 200 400 km

**Tungsten and Uranium**

- Tungsten
- Uranium

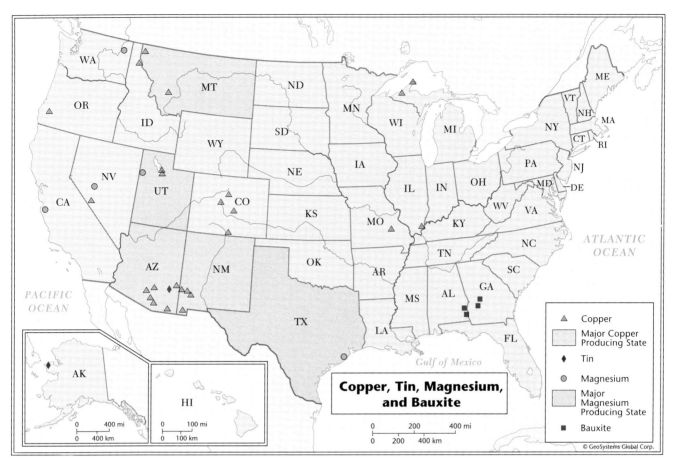

## Copper, Tin, Magnesium, and Bauxite

WA
OR
CA
NV
ID
MT
WY
UT
CO
AZ
NM
ND
SD
NE
KS
OK
TX
MN
IA
MO
AR
LA
WI
IL
MI
IN
OH
KY
TN
MS
AL
GA
FL
SC
NC
VA
WV
PA
NY
MD
DE
NJ
CT
RI
MA
VT
NH
ME
AK
HI
PACIFIC OCEAN
ATLANTIC OCEAN
Gulf of Mexico

- Copper
- Major Copper Producing State
- Tin
- Magnesium
- Major Magnesium Producing State
- Bauxite

0 400 mi
0 400 km
0 100 mi
0 100 km
0 200 400 mi
0 200 400 km



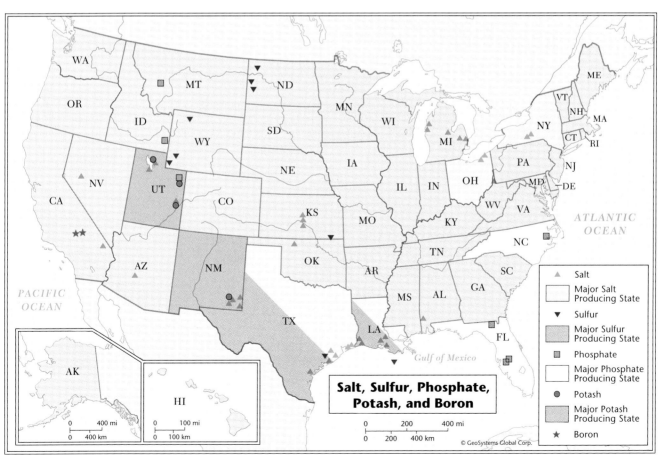

## Salt, Sulfur, Phosphate, Potash, and Boron

WA
OR
CA
NV
ID
MT
WY
UT
CO
AZ
NM
ND
SD
NE
KS
OK
TX
MN
IA
MO
AR
LA
WI
IL
MI
IN
OH
KY
TN
MS
AL
GA
FL
SC
NC
VA
WV
PA
NY
MD
DE
NJ
CT
RI
MA
VT
NH
ME
AK
HI
PACIFIC OCEAN
ATLANTIC OCEAN
Gulf of Mexico

- Salt
- Major Salt Producing State
- Sulfur
- Major Sulfur Producing State
- Phosphate
- Major Phosphate Producing State
- Potash
- Major Potash Producing State
- Boron

0 400 mi
0 400 km
0 100 mi
0 100 km
0 200 400 mi
0 200 400 km

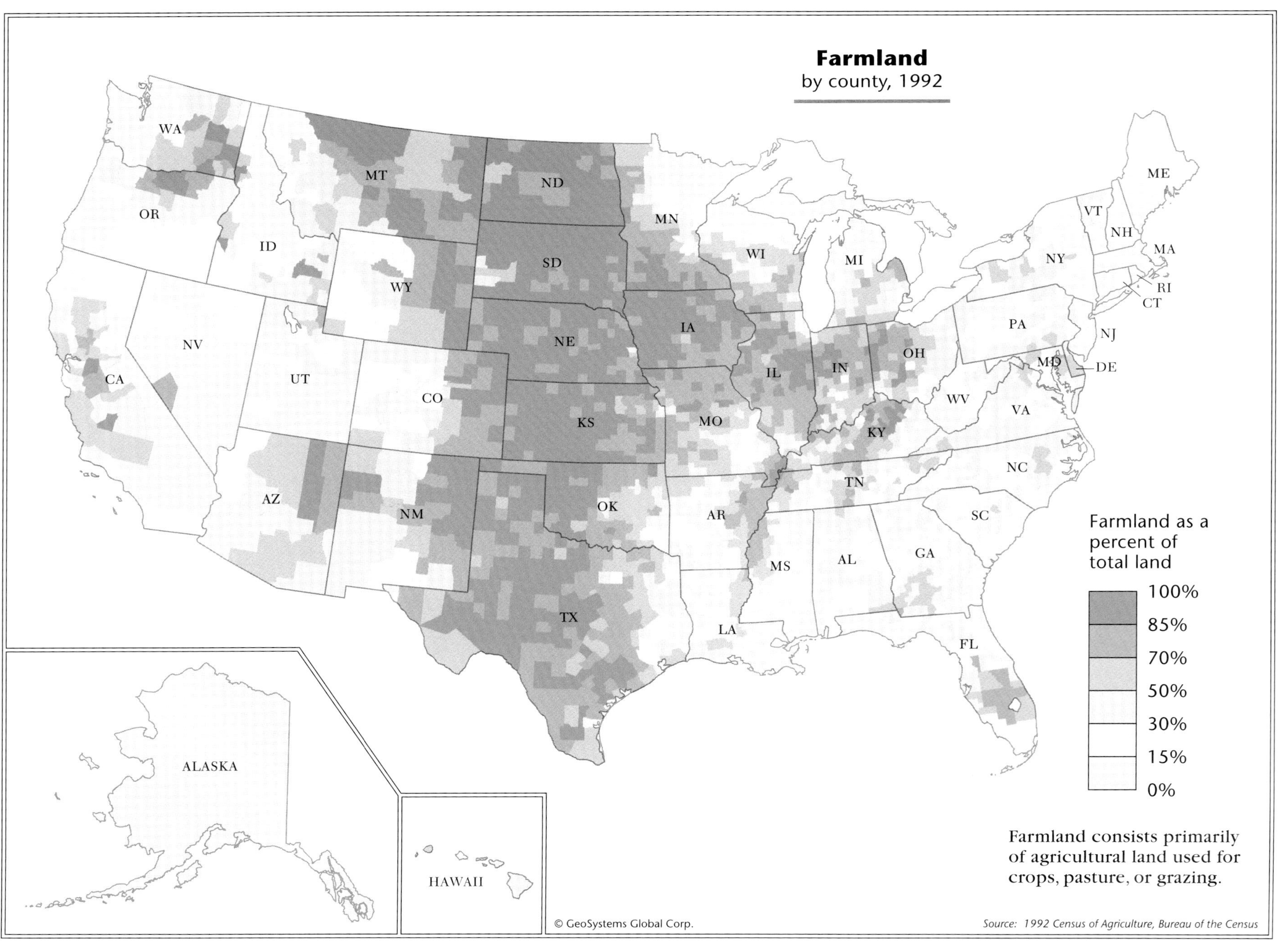
Farmland
by county, 1992
Farmland as a percent of total land
100%
85%
70%
50%
30%
15%
0%
Farmland consists primarily of agricultural land used for crops, pasture, or grazing.
Source: 1992 Census of Agriculture, Bureau of the Census
© GeoSystems Global Corp.
ME
VT
NH
MA
RI
CT
NY
NJ
DE
PA
MD
VA
NC
SC
WV
FL
OH
GA
KY
MI
IN
TN
AL
IL
MS
WI
AR
LA
MO
IA
MN
OK
ND
SD
NE
KS
TX
MT
WY
CO
NM
ID
UT
AZ
WA
OR
NV
CA
HAWAII
ALASKA

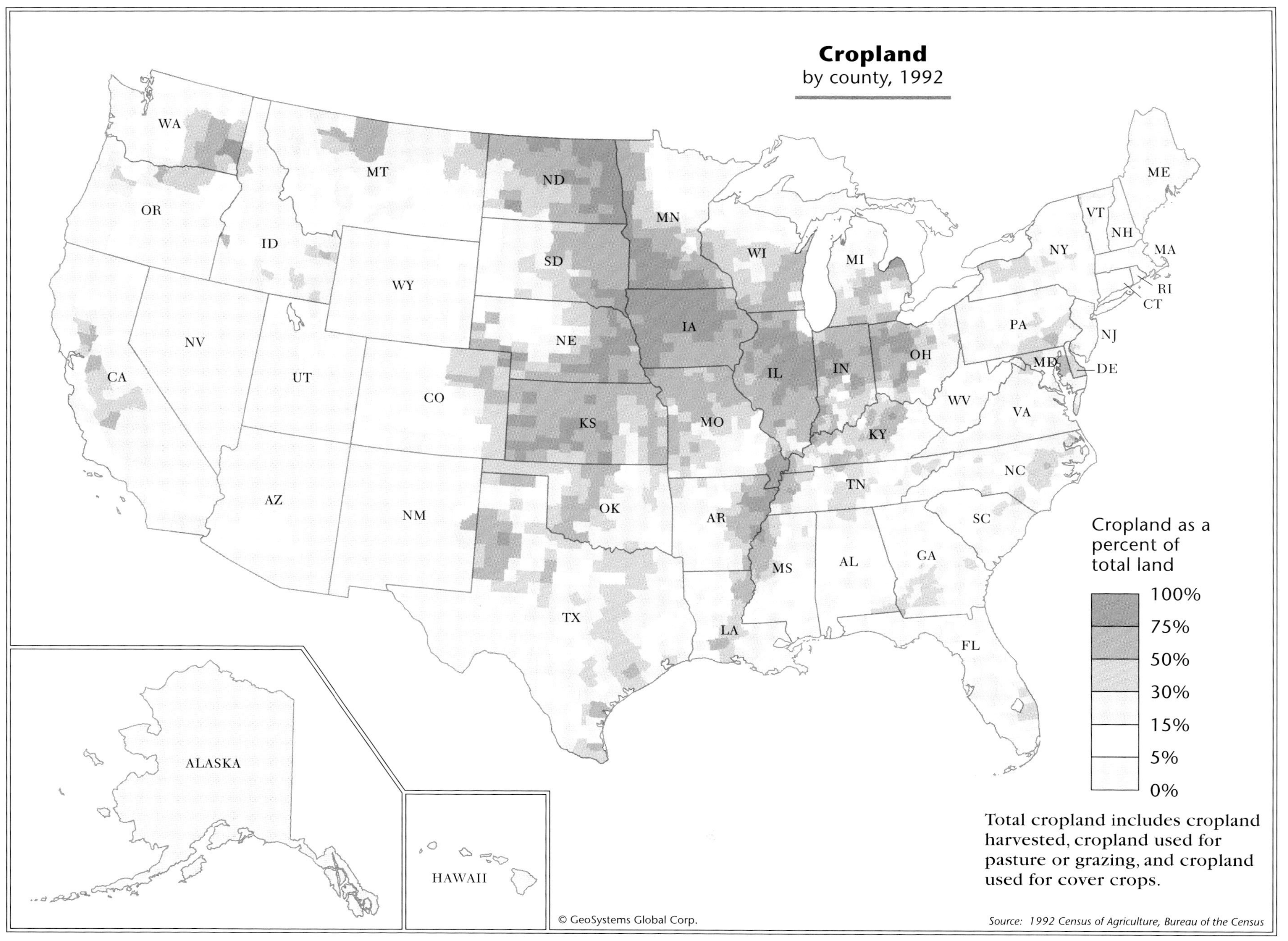

Cropland
by county, 1992
WA
OR
CA
ID
NV
MT
WY
UT
AZ
CO
NM
ND
SD
NE
KS
OK
TX
MN
IA
MO
AR
LA
WI
IL
MS
MI
IN
KY
TN
AL
OH
WV
GA
FL
PA
NY
VA
NC
SC
MD
DE
NJ
VT
NH
ME
MA
RI
CT
ALASKA
HAWAII
Cropland as a percent of total land
100%
75%
50%
30%
15%
5%
0%
Total cropland includes cropland harvested, cropland used for pasture or grazing, and cropland used for cover crops.
© GeoSystems Global Corp.
Source: 1992 Census of Agriculture, Bureau of the Census

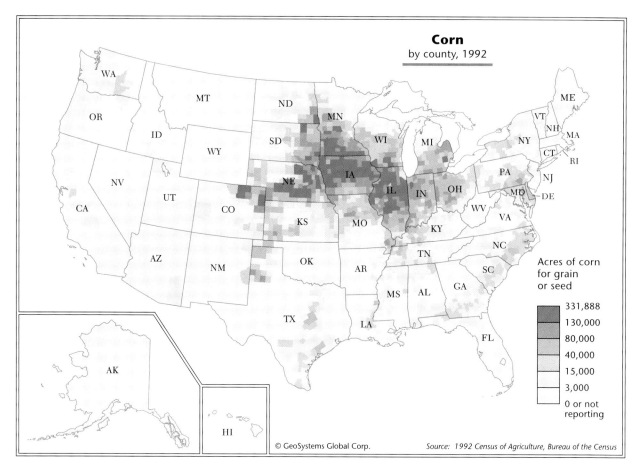

## Corn
by county, 1992

Acres of corn for grain or seed

331,888
130,000
80,000
40,000
15,000
3,000
0 or not reporting



*Source: 1992 Census of Agriculture, Bureau of the Census*

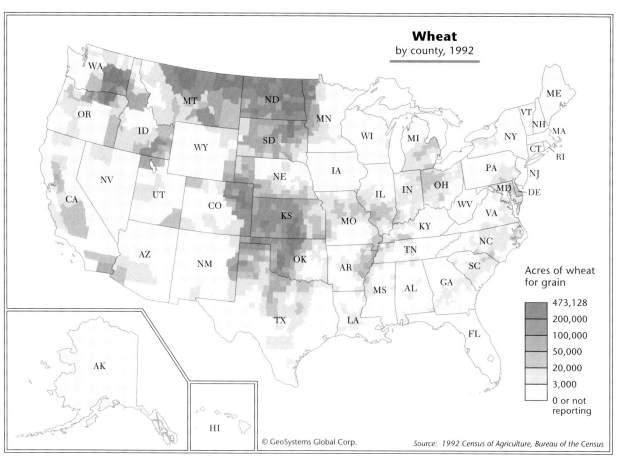

## Wheat
by county, 1992

Acres of wheat for grain

473,128
200,000
100,000
50,000
20,000
3,000
0 or not reporting



*Source: 1992 Census of Agriculture, Bureau of the Census*

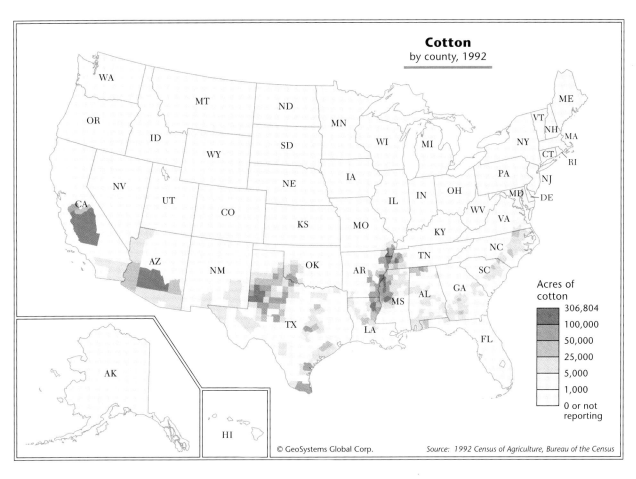

## Cotton
by county, 1992

Acres of cotton

- 306,804
- 100,000
- 50,000
- 25,000
- 5,000
- 1,000
- 0 or not reporting



*Source: 1992 Census of Agriculture, Bureau of the Census*

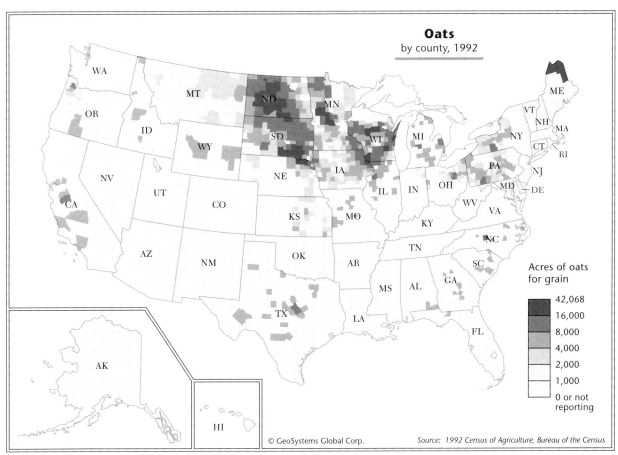

## Oats
by county, 1992

Acres of oats for grain

- 42,068
- 16,000
- 8,000
- 4,000
- 2,000
- 1,000
- 0 or not reporting



*Source: 1992 Census of Agriculture, Bureau of the Census*

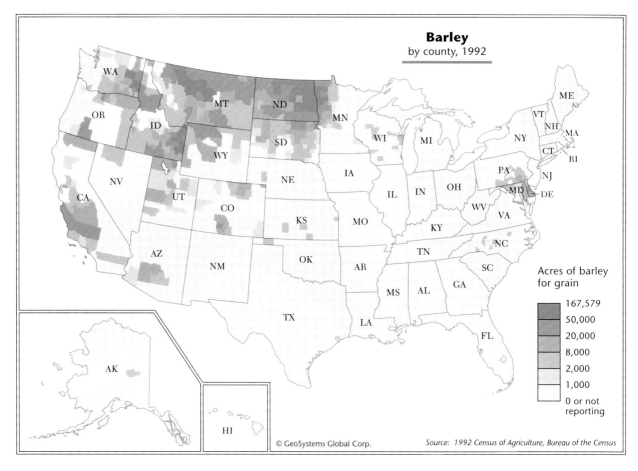

## Barley
by county, 1992

Acres of barley for grain

- 167,579
- 50,000
- 20,000
- 8,000
- 2,000
- 1,000
- 0 or not reporting



*Source: 1992 Census of Agriculture, Bureau of the Census*

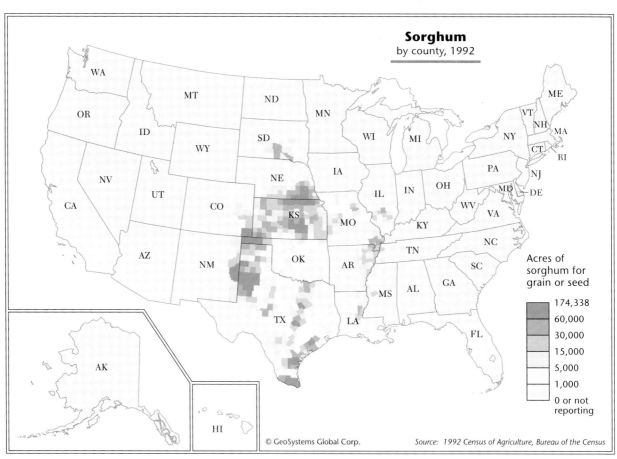

## Sorghum
by county, 1992

Acres of sorghum for grain or seed

- 174,338
- 60,000
- 30,000
- 15,000
- 5,000
- 1,000
- 0 or not reporting



*Source: 1992 Census of Agriculture, Bureau of the Census*

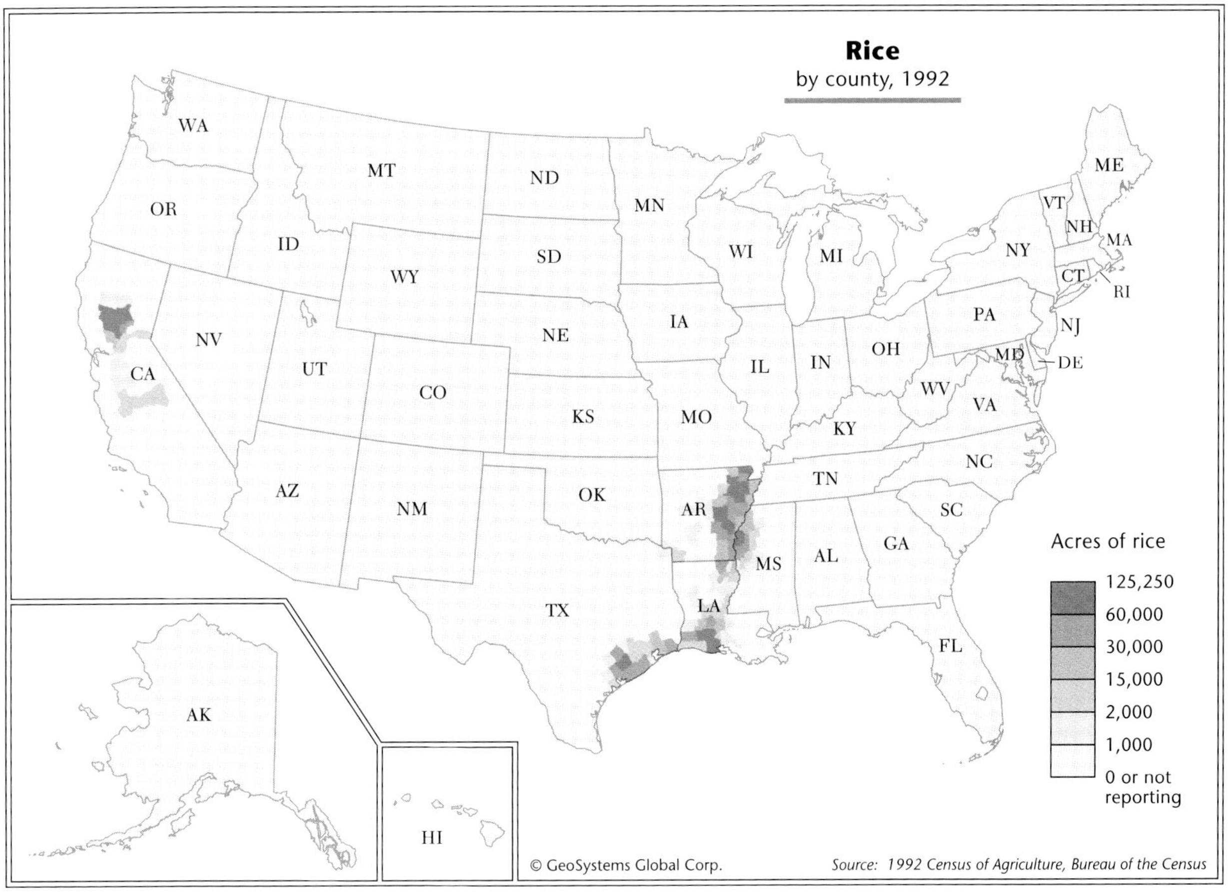
Rice
by county, 1992
WA
OR
CA
NV
ID
MT
WY
UT
AZ
NM
CO
ND
SD
NE
KS
OK
TX
MN
IA
MO
AR
LA
WI
IL
MI
IN
OH
KY
TN
MS
AL
GA
FL
SC
NC
VA
WV
PA
NY
VT
NH
ME
MA
CT
RI
NJ
MD
DE
AK
HI
Acres of rice
125,250
60,000
30,000
15,000
2,000
1,000
0 or not reporting
© GeoSystems Global Corp.
Source: 1992 Census of Agriculture, Bureau of the Census

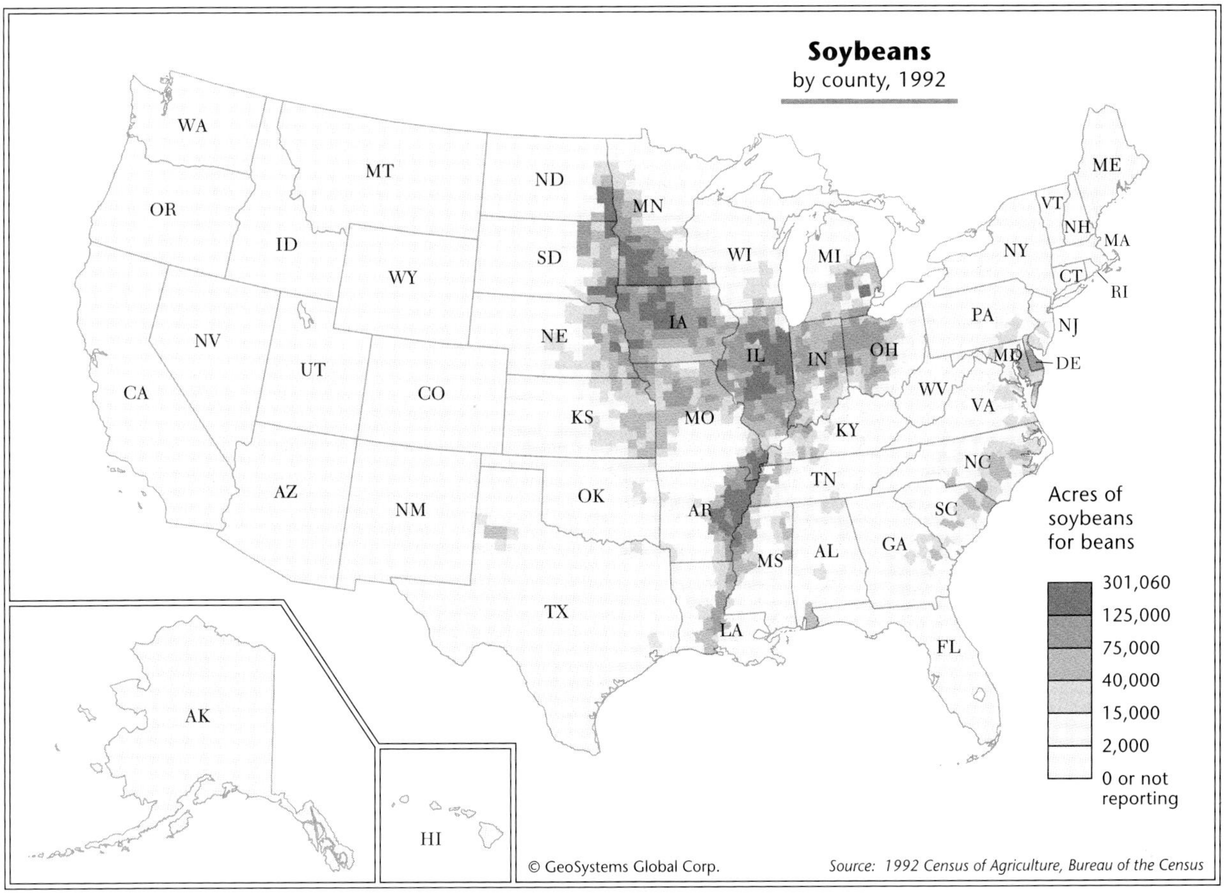
Soybeans
by county, 1992
WA
OR
CA
NV
ID
MT
WY
UT
AZ
NM
CO
ND
SD
NE
KS
OK
TX
MN
IA
MO
AR
LA
WI
IL
MI
IN
OH
KY
TN
MS
AL
GA
FL
SC
NC
VA
WV
PA
NY
VT
NH
ME
MA
CT
RI
NJ
MD
DE
AK
HI
Acres of soybeans for beans
301,060
125,000
75,000
40,000
15,000
2,000
0 or not reporting
© GeoSystems Global Corp.
Source: 1992 Census of Agriculture, Bureau of the Census

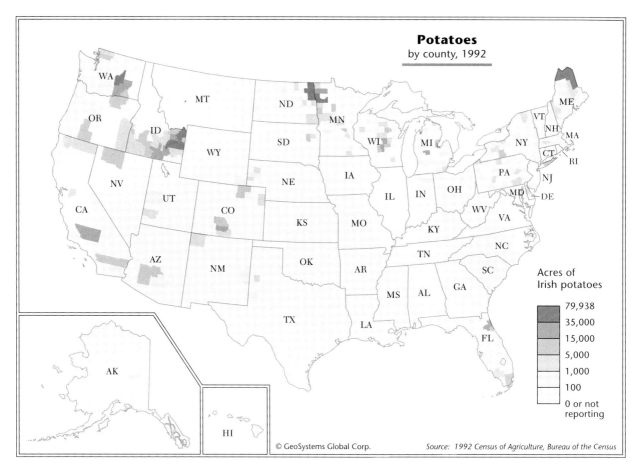

## Potatoes
by county, 1992

WA OR ID MT ND MN SD WY NV CA UT CO NE KS IA MO IL IN OH MI WI AZ NM OK TX AR LA MS AL GA TN KY NC SC FL VA WV MD DE NJ PA NY CT RI MA NH VT ME AK HI

Acres of Irish potatoes

- 79,938
- 35,000
- 15,000
- 5,000
- 1,000
- 100
- 0 or not reporting



*Source: 1992 Census of Agriculture, Bureau of the Census*

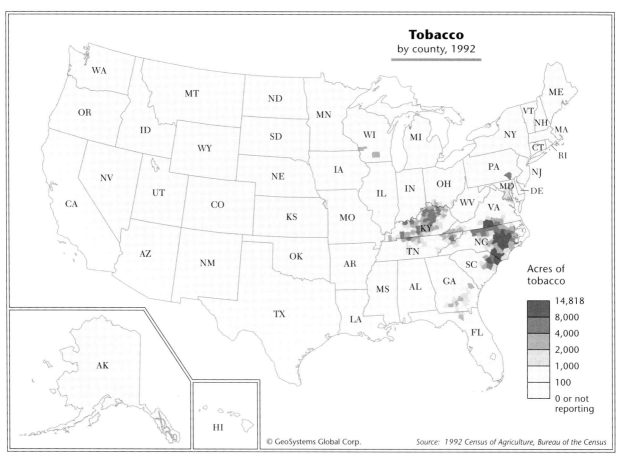

## Tobacco
by county, 1992

WA OR ID MT ND MN SD WY NV CA UT CO NE KS IA MO IL IN OH MI WI AZ NM OK TX AR LA MS AL GA TN KY NC SC FL VA WV MD DE NJ PA NY CT RI MA NH VT ME AK HI

Acres of tobacco

- 14,818
- 8,000
- 4,000
- 2,000
- 1,000
- 100
- 0 or not reporting



*Source: 1992 Census of Agriculture, Bureau of the Census*

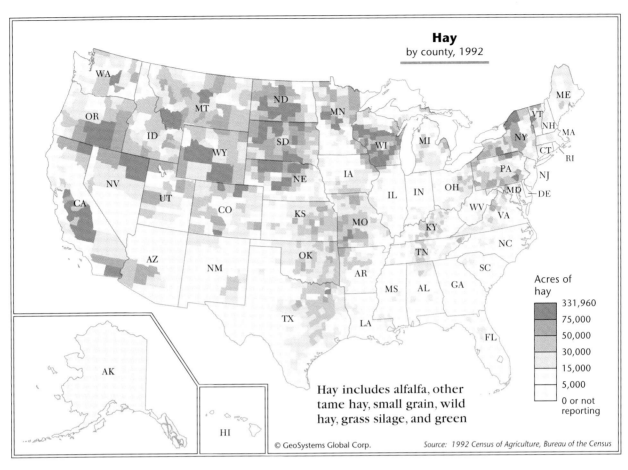

## Hay
by county, 1992

Acres of hay

- 331,960
- 75,000
- 50,000
- 30,000
- 15,000
- 5,000
- 0 or not reporting

Hay includes alfalfa, other tame hay, small grain, wild hay, grass silage, and green



*Source: 1992 Census of Agriculture, Bureau of the Census*

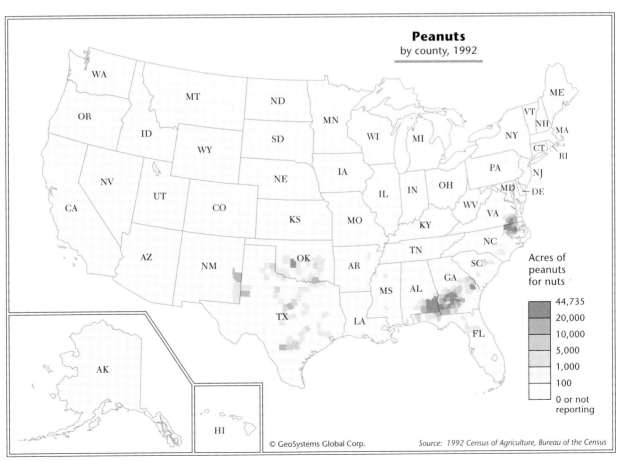

## Peanuts
by county, 1992

Acres of peanuts for nuts

- 44,735
- 20,000
- 10,000
- 5,000
- 1,000
- 100
- 0 or not reporting



*Source: 1992 Census of Agriculture, Bureau of the Census*

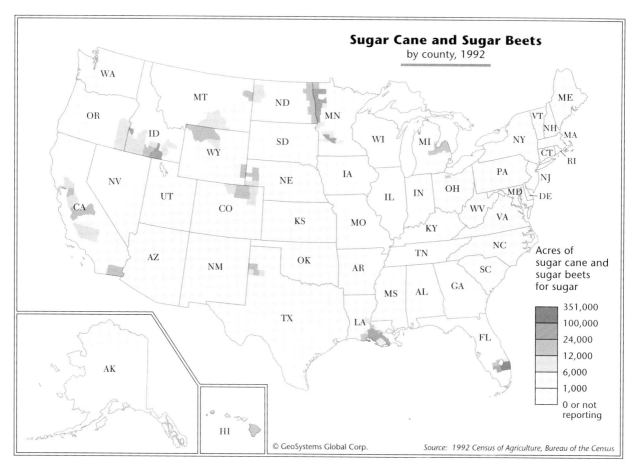

## Sugar Cane and Sugar Beets
by county, 1992

Acres of sugar cane and sugar beets for sugar

- 351,000
- 100,000
- 24,000
- 12,000
- 6,000
- 1,000
- 0 or not reporting



*Source: 1992 Census of Agriculture, Bureau of the Census*

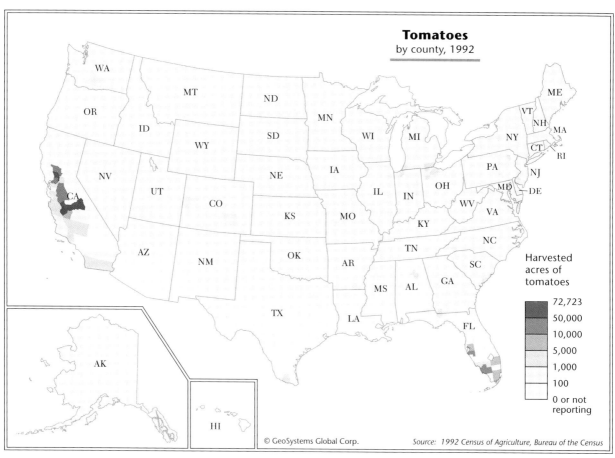

## Tomatoes
by county, 1992

Harvested acres of tomatoes

- 72,723
- 50,000
- 10,000
- 5,000
- 1,000
- 100
- 0 or not reporting



*Source: 1992 Census of Agriculture, Bureau of the Census*

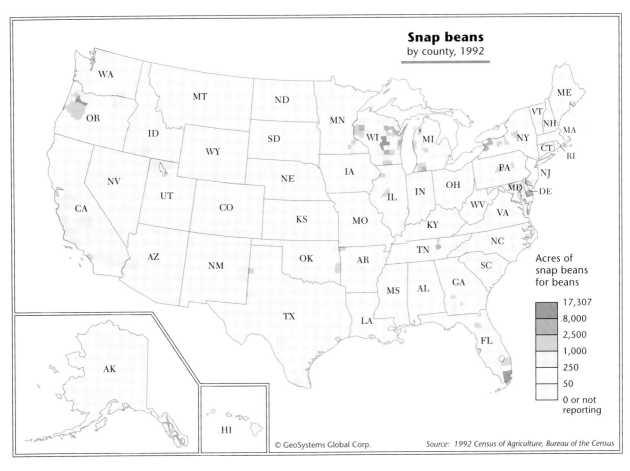

## Snap beans
by county, 1992



© GeoSystems Global Corp.

*Source: 1992 Census of Agriculture, Bureau of the Census*

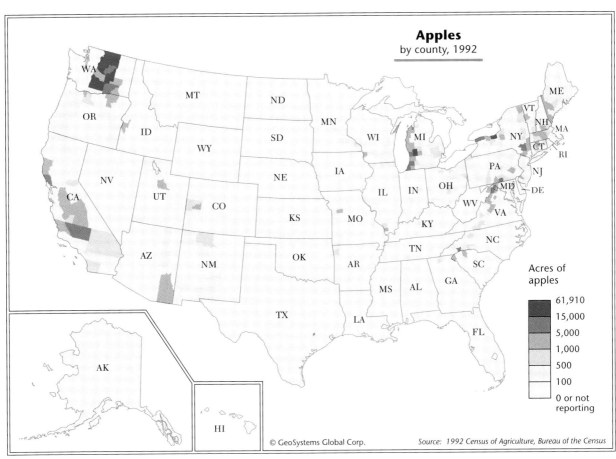

## Apples
by county, 1992



© GeoSystems Global Corp.

*Source: 1992 Census of Agriculture, Bureau of the Census*

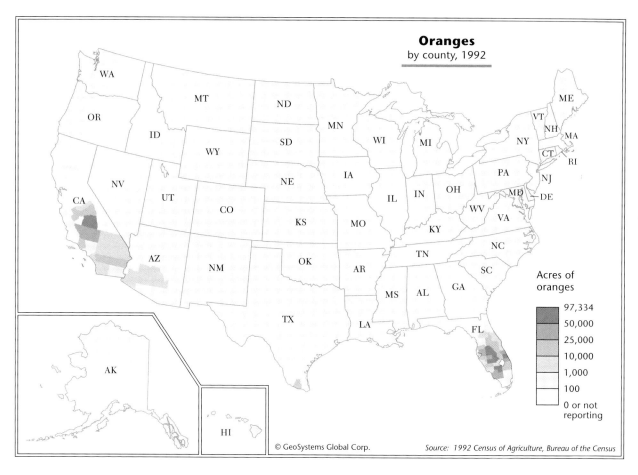

## Oranges
by county, 1992

Acres of oranges

- 97,334
- 50,000
- 25,000
- 10,000
- 1,000
- 100
- 0 or not reporting



*Source: 1992 Census of Agriculture, Bureau of the Census*

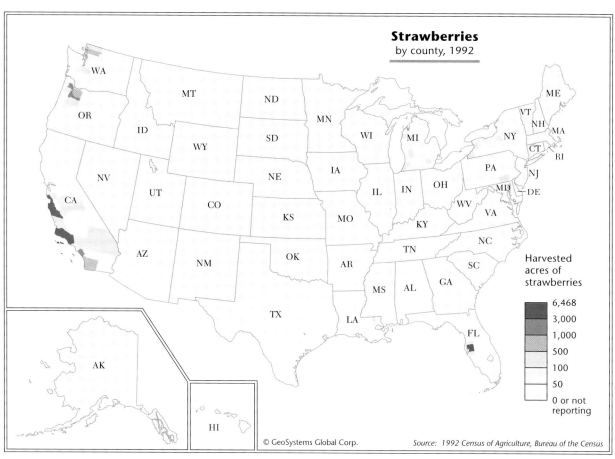

## Strawberries
by county, 1992

Harvested acres of strawberries

- 6,468
- 3,000
- 1,000
- 500
- 100
- 50
- 0 or not reporting



*Source: 1992 Census of Agriculture, Bureau of the Census*

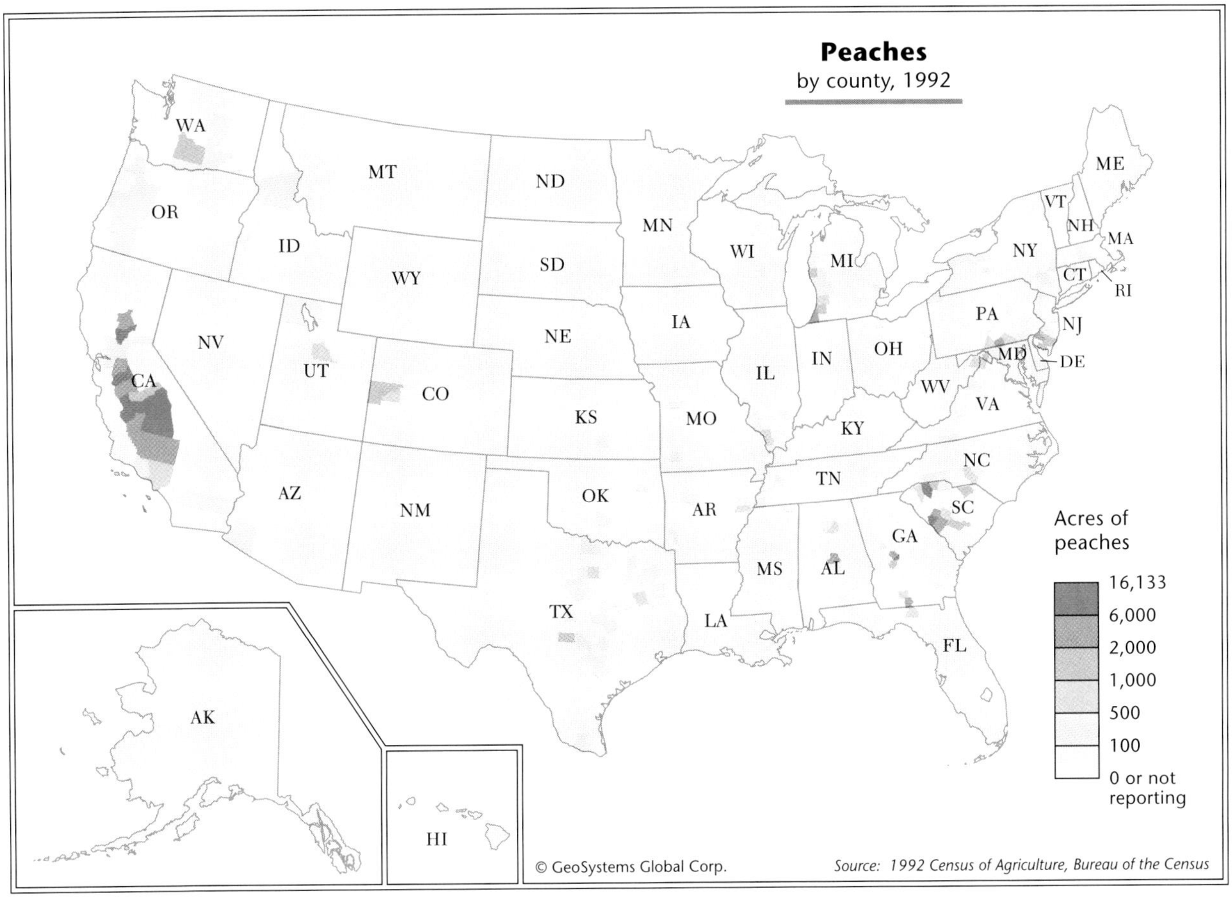
Peaches
by county, 1992
WA
OR
MT
ND
MN
ID
SD
WI
MI
NY
ME
VT
NH
MA
CT
RI
WY
IA
PA
NJ
NE
NV
CA
UT
CO
IN
OH
MD
DE
IL
WV
VA
KS
MO
KY
NC
TN
AZ
NM
OK
AR
SC
GA
MS
AL
TX
LA
FL
AK
HI
Acres of peaches
16,133
6,000
2,000
1,000
500
100
0 or not reporting
© GeoSystems Global Corp.
Source: 1992 Census of Agriculture, Bureau of the Census

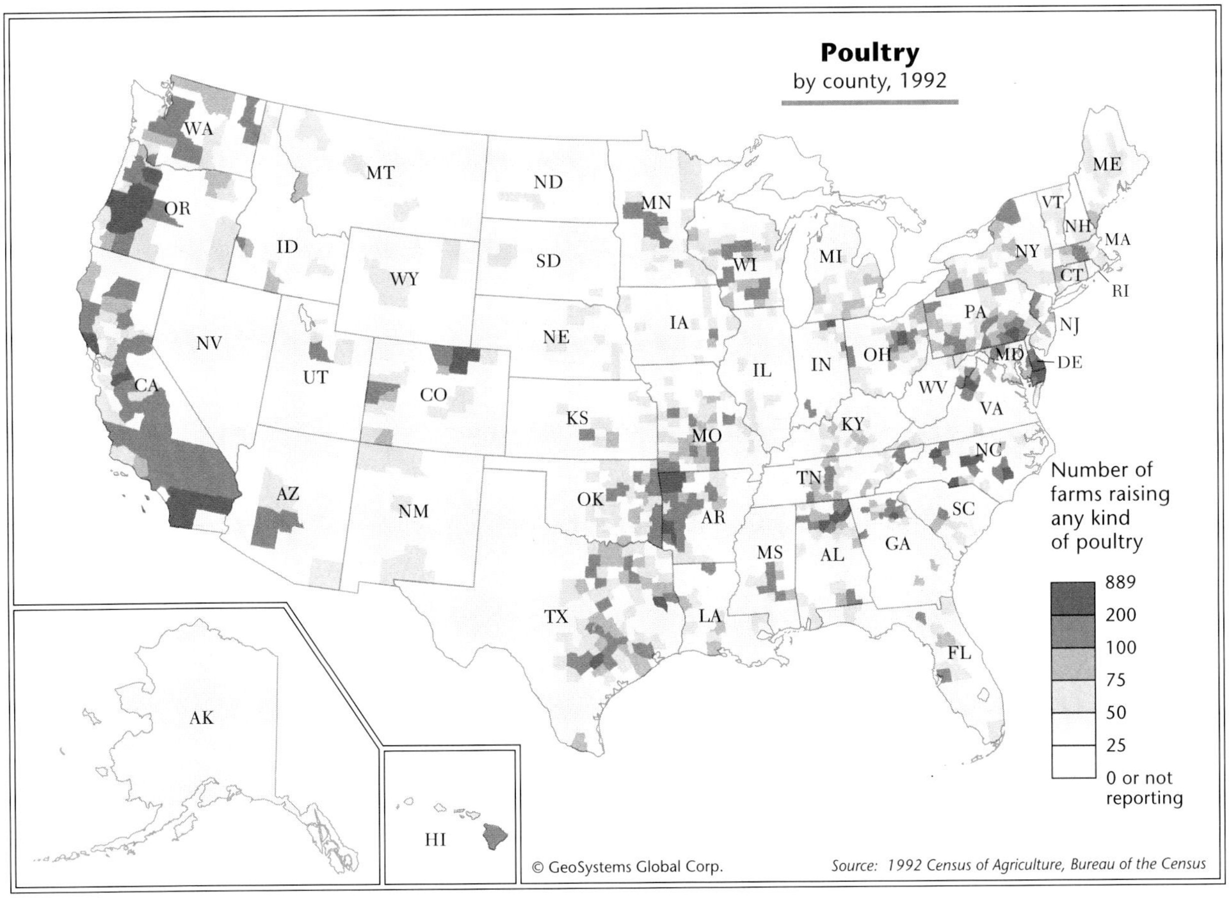
Poultry
by county, 1992
WA
OR
MT
ND
MN
ID
SD
WI
MI
NY
ME
VT
NH
MA
CT
RI
WY
IA
PA
NJ
NE
NV
CA
UT
CO
IN
OH
MD
DE
IL
WV
VA
KS
MO
KY
NC
TN
AZ
NM
OK
AR
SC
GA
MS
AL
TX
LA
FL
AK
HI
Number of farms raising any kind of poultry
889
200
100
75
50
25
0 or not reporting
© GeoSystems Global Corp.
Source: 1992 Census of Agriculture, Bureau of the Census

## Beef Cows

by county, 1992

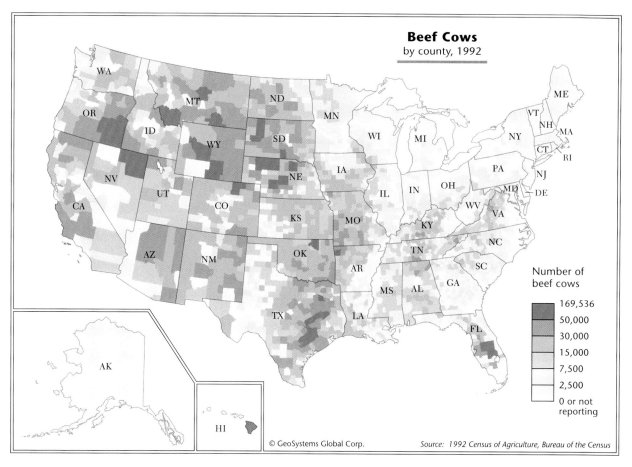

Number of beef cows

- 169,536
- 50,000
- 30,000
- 15,000
- 7,500
- 2,500
- 0 or not reporting



*Source: 1992 Census of Agriculture, Bureau of the Census*

## Dairy Cows

by county, 1992

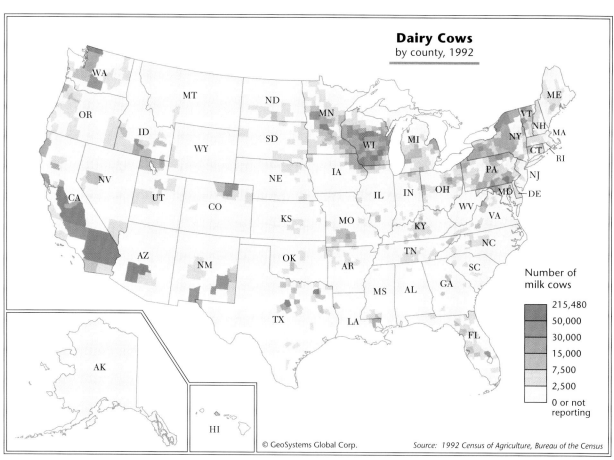

Number of milk cows

- 215,480
- 50,000
- 30,000
- 15,000
- 7,500
- 2,500
- 0 or not reporting



*Source: 1992 Census of Agriculture, Bureau of the Census*

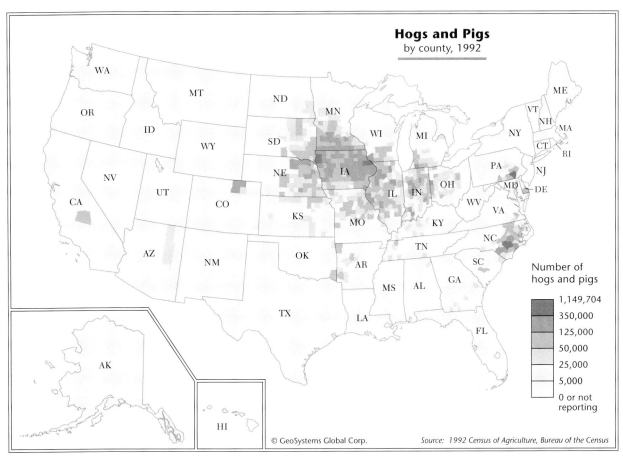

## Hogs and Pigs
by county, 1992

Number of hogs and pigs
1,149,704
350,000
125,000
50,000
25,000
5,000
0 or not reporting



*Source: 1992 Census of Agriculture, Bureau of the Census*

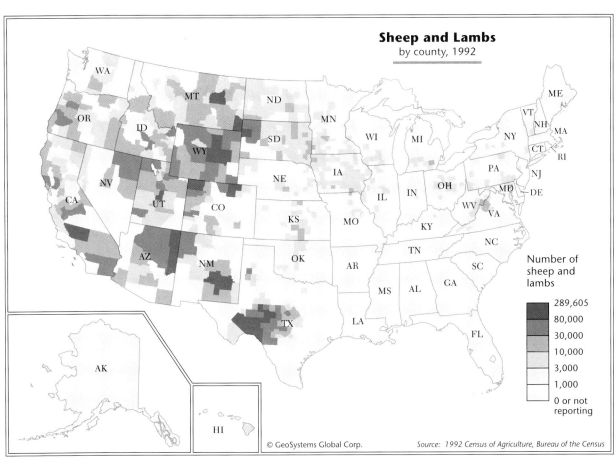

## Sheep and Lambs
by county, 1992

Number of sheep and lambs
289,605
80,000
30,000
10,000
3,000
1,000
0 or not reporting



*Source: 1992 Census of Agriculture, Bureau of the Census*

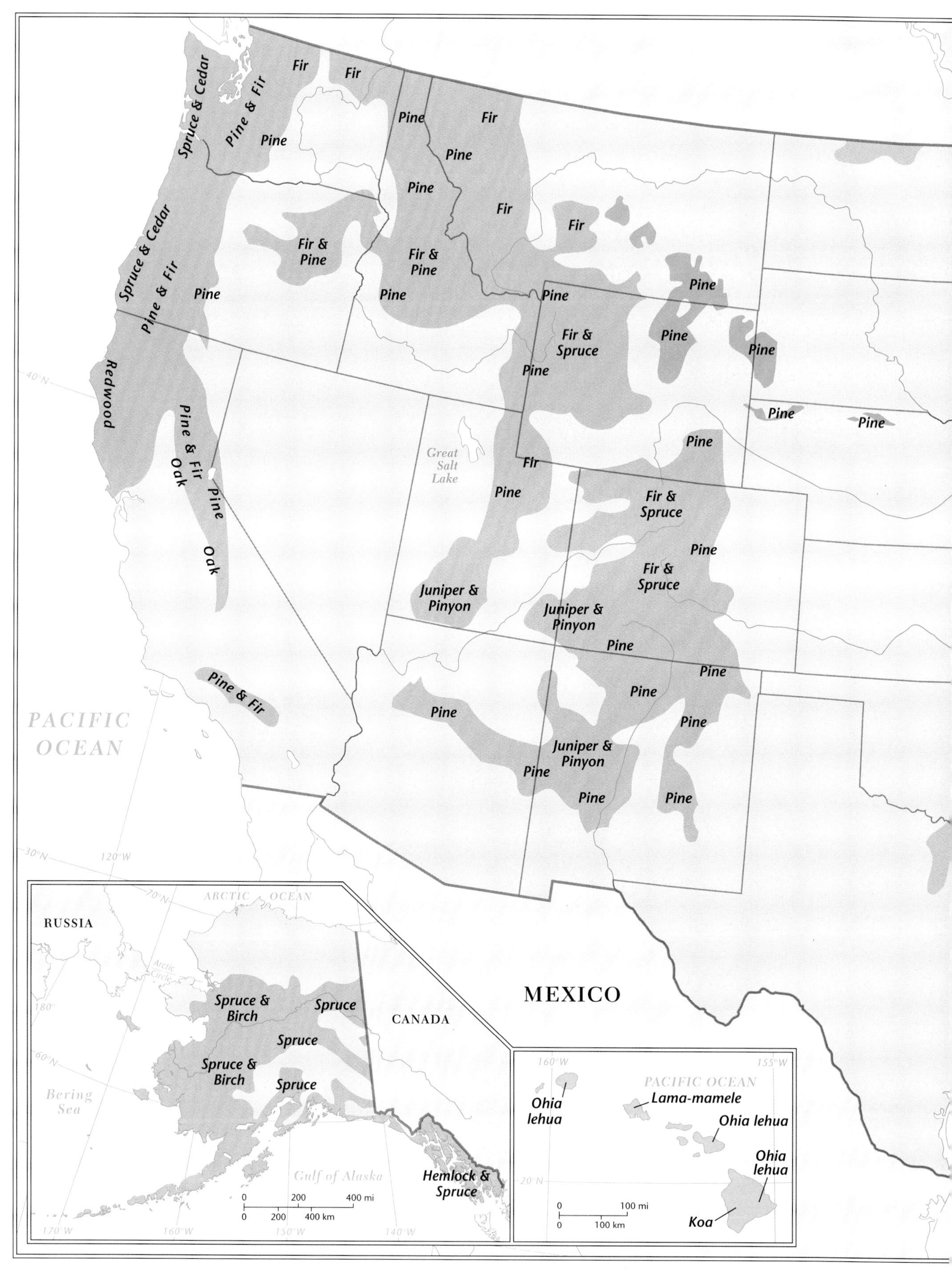

Fir
Fir
Spruce & Cedar
Pine & Fir
Pine
Pine
Fir
Pine
Pine
Fir
Fir
Fir & Pine
Fir & Pine
Spruce & Cedar
Pine & Fir
Pine
Pine
Pine
Pine
Fir & Spruce
Pine
Pine
Pine
Pine
Pine
Redwood
Pine & Fir
Oak
Pine
Oak
Great Salt Lake
Fir
Pine
Pine
Fir & Spruce
Pine
Fir & Spruce
Juniper & Pinyon
Juniper & Pinyon
Pine
Pine
Pine & Fir
Pine
Pine
Pine
Juniper & Pinyon
Pine
Pine
Pine
PACIFIC OCEAN
MEXICO
ARCTIC OCEAN
RUSSIA
Arctic Circle
Spruce & Birch
Spruce
CANADA
Spruce
Spruce & Birch
Spruce
Bering Sea
Gulf of Alaska
Hemlock & Spruce
0 200 400 mi
0 200 400 km
PACIFIC OCEAN
Ohia lehua
Lama-mamele
Ohia lehua
Ohia lehua
Koa
0 100 mi
0 100 km

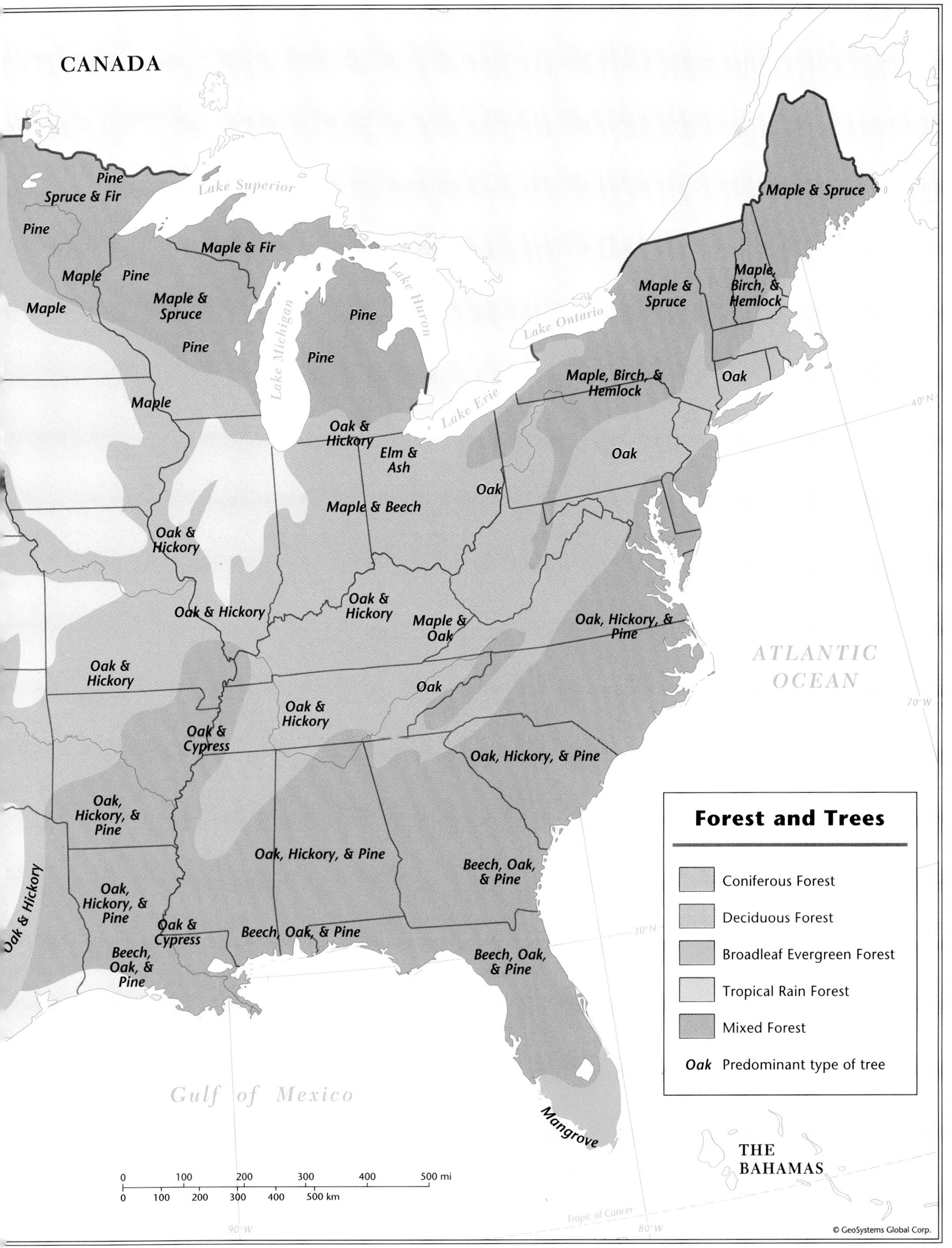
CANADA
Lake Superior
Lake Michigan
Lake Huron
Lake Ontario
Lake Erie
ATLANTIC OCEAN
Gulf of Mexico
THE BAHAMAS
Pine
Spruce & Fir
Pine
Maple
Pine
Maple
Maple & Fir
Maple & Spruce
Pine
Pine
Pine
Maple
Oak & Hickory
Elm & Ash
Maple & Beech
Oak
Oak & Hickory
Oak & Hickory
Oak & Hickory
Maple & Oak
Oak & Hickory
Oak
Oak & Hickory
Oak & Cypress
Oak, Hickory, & Pine
Oak, Hickory, & Pine
Oak, Hickory, & Pine
Oak & Hickory
Oak, Hickory, & Pine
Oak & Cypress
Beech, Oak, & Pine
Beech, Oak, & Pine
Beech, Oak, & Pine
Beech, Oak, & Pine
Oak, Hickory, & Pine
Mangrove
Maple & Spruce
Maple, Birch, & Hemlock
Maple & Spruce
Maple, Birch, & Hemlock
Oak
Oak
Forest and Trees
Coniferous Forest
Deciduous Forest
Broadleaf Evergreen Forest
Tropical Rain Forest
Mixed Forest
Oak Predominant type of tree
0 100 200 300 400 500 mi
0 100 200 300 400 500 km
40°N
30°N
70°W
80°W
90°W
Tropic of Cancer
© GeoSystems Global Corp.

# National Park System

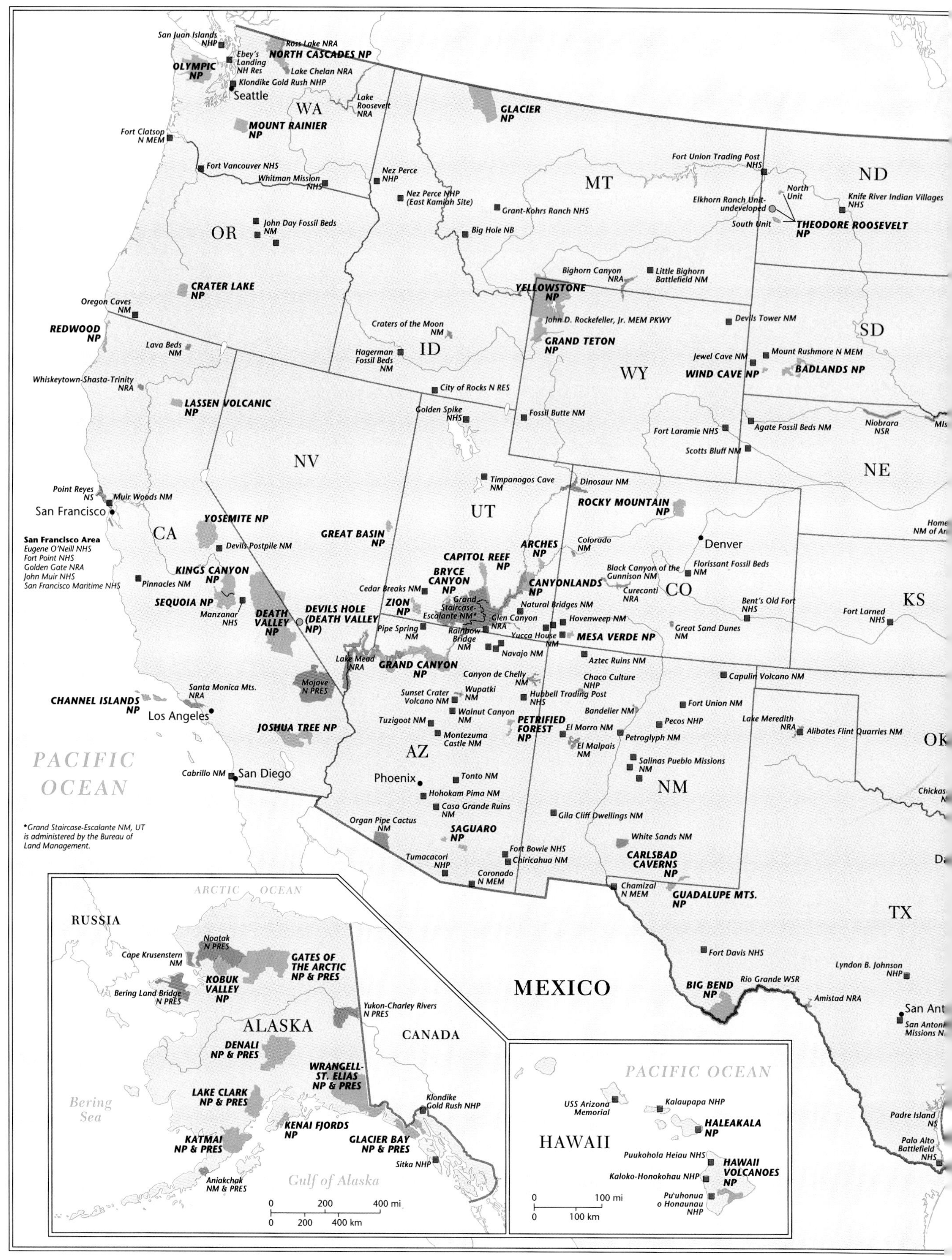

San Juan Islands NHP
Ross Lake NRA
Ebey's Landing NH Res
NORTH CASCADES NP
OLYMPIC NP
Lake Chelan NRA
Klondike Gold Rush NHP
Seattle
WA
Lake Roosevelt NRA
GLACIER NP
Fort Clatsop N MEM
MOUNT RAINIER NP
Fort Vancouver NHS
Whitman Mission NHS
Nez Perce NHP
Nez Perce NHP (East Kamiah Site)
MT
Fort Union Trading Post NHS
ND
North Unit
Elkhorn Ranch Unit-undeveloped
South Unit
THEODORE ROOSEVELT NP
Knife River Indian Villages NHS
Grant-Kohrs Ranch NHS
John Day Fossil Beds NM
OR
Big Hole NB
Bighorn Canyon NRA
Little Bighorn Battlefield NM
CRATER LAKE NP
YELLOWSTONE NP
Oregon Caves NM
REDWOOD NP
Craters of the Moon NM
John D. Rockefeller, Jr. MEM PKWY
Devils Tower NM
SD
GRAND TETON NP
Lava Beds NM
Hagerman Fossil Beds NM
ID
Jewel Cave NM
Mount Rushmore N MEM
WY
WIND CAVE NP
BADLANDS NP
Whiskeytown-Shasta-Trinity NRA
City of Rocks N RES
LASSEN VOLCANIC NP
Golden Spike NHS
Fossil Butte NM
Fort Laramie NHS
Agate Fossil Beds NM
Niobrara NSR
Scotts Bluff NM
NV
NE
Point Reyes NS
Muir Woods NM
San Francisco
Timpanogos Cave NM
Dinosaur NM
ROCKY MOUNTAIN NP
UT
YOSEMITE NP
CA
San Francisco Area
Eugene O'Neill NHS
Fort Point NHS
Golden Gate NRA
John Muir NHS
San Francisco Maritime NHS
Devils Postpile NM
GREAT BASIN NP
Denver
Colorado NM
ARCHES NP
CAPITOL REEF NP
KINGS CANYON NP
Pinnacles NM
BRYCE CANYON NP
Black Canyon of the Gunnison NM
Florissant Fossil Beds NM
Cedar Breaks NM
CANYONLANDS NP
CO
Curecanti NRA
SEQUOIA NP
ZION NP
Grand Staircase-Escalante NM*
Natural Bridges NM
Bent's Old Fort NHS
KS
Manzanar NHS
DEATH VALLEY NP
DEVILS HOLE (DEATH VALLEY NP)
Glen Canyon NRA
Hovenweep NM
Fort Larned NHS
Pipe Spring NM
Rainbow Bridge NM
Yucca House NM
MESA VERDE NP
Great Sand Dunes NM
Navajo NM
Lake Mead NRA
Aztec Ruins NM
GRAND CANYON NP
Canyon de Chelly NM
Chaco Culture NHP
Capulin Volcano NM
Mojave N PRES
Santa Monica Mts. NRA
Sunset Crater Volcano NM
Wupatki NM
Hubbell Trading Post NHS
CHANNEL ISLANDS NP
Fort Union NM
Los Angeles
Walnut Canyon NM
Bandelier NM
Tuzigoot NM
PETRIFIED FOREST NP
Pecos NHP
Lake Meredith NRA
Alibates Flint Quarries NM
JOSHUA TREE NP
Montezuma Castle NM
El Morro NM
Petroglyph NM
AZ
El Malpais NM
PACIFIC OCEAN
Salinas Pueblo Missions NM
Cabrillo NM
San Diego
Phoenix
Tonto NM
NM
Hohokam Pima NM
Casa Grande Ruins NM
*Grand Staircase-Escalante NM, UT is administered by the Bureau of Land Management.
Gila Cliff Dwellings NM
Organ Pipe Cactus NM
SAGUARO NP
White Sands NM
Fort Bowie NHS
Chiricahua NM
CARLSBAD CAVERNS NP
Tumacacori NHP
Coronado N MEM
Chamizal N MEM
GUADALUPE MTS. NP
TX
ARCTIC OCEAN
RUSSIA
Noatak N PRES
Cape Krusenstern NM
GATES OF THE ARCTIC NP & PRES
KOBUK VALLEY NP
Bering Land Bridge N PRES
Yukon-Charley Rivers N PRES
ALASKA
CANADA
DENALI NP & PRES
WRANGELL-ST. ELIAS NP & PRES
Bering Sea
LAKE CLARK NP & PRES
Klondike Gold Rush NHP
KENAI FJORDS NP
KATMAI NP & PRES
GLACIER BAY NP & PRES
Sitka NHP
Aniakchak NM & PRES
Gulf of Alaska
0 200 400 mi
0 200 400 km
Fort Davis NHS
Lyndon B. Johnson NHP
MEXICO
BIG BEND NP
Rio Grande WSR
Amistad NRA
San Antonio Missions NHP
PACIFIC OCEAN
USS Arizona Memorial
Kalaupapa NHP
HALEAKALA NP
HAWAII
Puukohola Heiau NHS
HAWAII VOLCANOES NP
Kaloko-Honokohau NHP
Pu'uhonua o Honaunau NHP
0 100 mi
0 100 km
Padre Island NS
Palo Alto Battlefield NHS

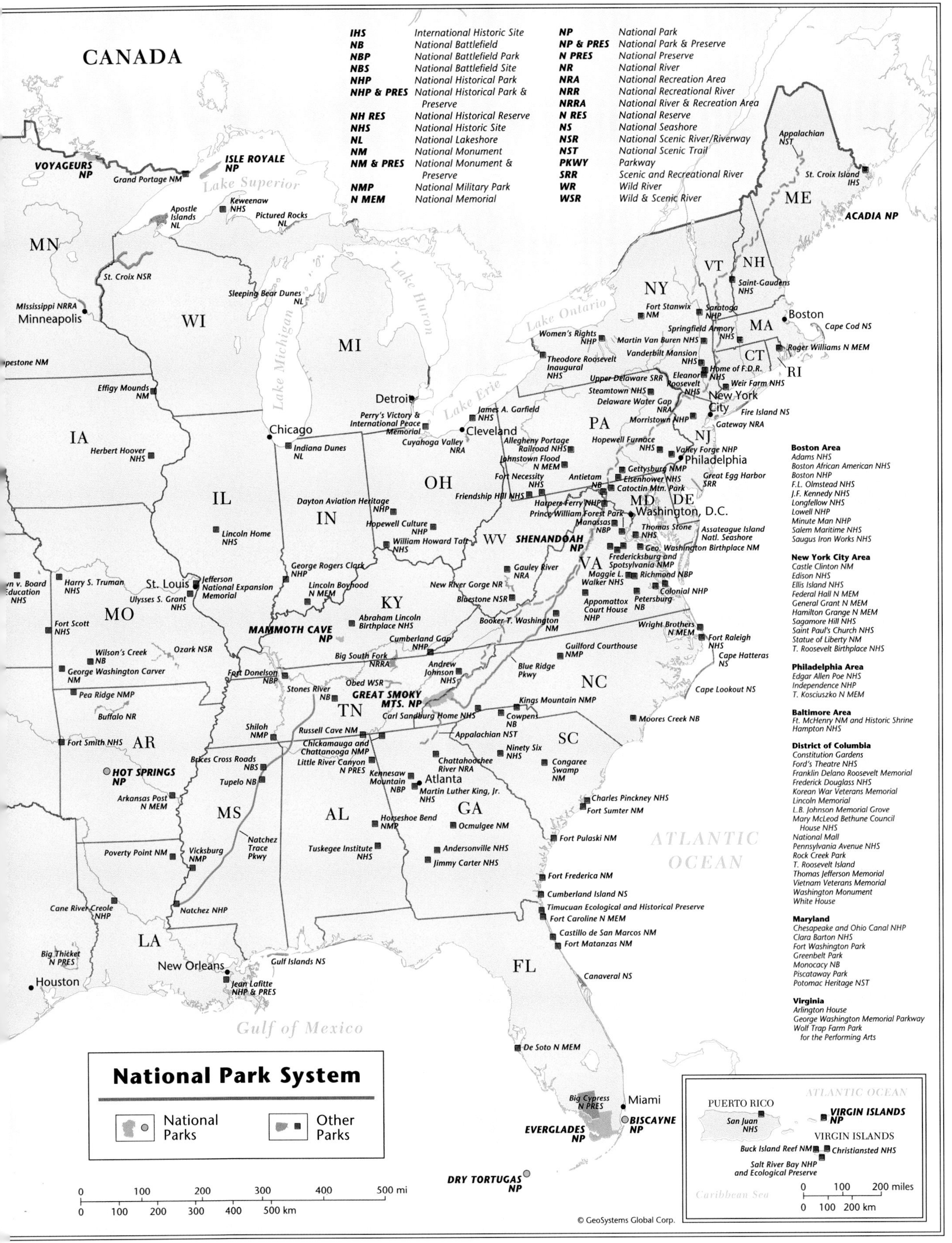

IHS International Historic Site
NB National Battlefield
NBP National Battlefield Park
NBS National Battlefield Site
NHP National Historical Park
NHP & PRES National Historical Park & Preserve
NH RES National Historical Reserve
NHS National Historic Site
NL National Lakeshore
NM National Monument
NM & PRES National Monument & Preserve
NMP National Military Park
N MEM National Memorial
NP National Park
NP & PRES National Park & Preserve
N PRES National Preserve
NR National River
NRA National Recreation Area
NRR National Recreational River
NRRA National River & Recreation Area
N RES National Reserve
NS National Seashore
NSR National Scenic River/Riverway
NST National Scenic Trail
PKWY Parkway
SRR Scenic and Recreational River
WR Wild River
WSR Wild & Scenic River
CANADA
VOYAGEURS NP
Grand Portage NM
ISLE ROYALE NP
Lake Superior
Keweenaw NHS
Apostle Islands NL
Pictured Rocks NL
MN
St. Croix NSR
Mississippi NRRA
Minneapolis
Sleeping Bear Dunes NL
WI
MI
Lake Michigan
Lake Huron
Lake Ontario
Lake Erie
Pipestone NM
Effigy Mounds NM
Detroit
Chicago
Cleveland
IA
Herbert Hoover NHS
Indiana Dunes NL
Perry's Victory & International Peace Memorial
James A. Garfield NHS
Cuyahoga Valley NRA
IL
IN
OH
Dayton Aviation Heritage NHP
Hopewell Culture NHP
William Howard Taft NHS
Lincoln Home NHS
George Rogers Clark NHP
St. Louis
Jefferson National Expansion Memorial
Ulysses S. Grant NHS
Harry S. Truman NHS
Brown v. Board of Education NHS
Fort Scott NHS
MO
Lincoln Boyhood N MEM
KY
Abraham Lincoln Birthplace NHS
MAMMOTH CAVE NP
Wilson's Creek NB
Ozark NSR
George Washington Carver NM
Pea Ridge NMP
Buffalo NR
Fort Smith NHS
AR
HOT SPRINGS NP
Arkansas Post N MEM
Poverty Point NM
Cane River Creole NHP
LA
Big Thicket N PRES
Houston
New Orleans
Jean Lafitte NHP & PRES
Gulf Islands NS
Gulf of Mexico
Fort Donelson NBP
Stones River NB
Shiloh NMP
Brices Cross Roads NBS
Tupelo NB
MS
Vicksburg NMP
Natchez Trace Pkwy
Natchez NHP
TN
Big South Fork NRRA
Obed WSR
GREAT SMOKY MTS. NP
Cumberland Gap NHP
Andrew Johnson NHS
Russell Cave NM
Chickamauga and Chattanooga NMP
Little River Canyon N PRES
AL
Kennesaw Mountain NBP
Atlanta
Martin Luther King, Jr. NHS
Horseshoe Bend NMP
Tuskegee Institute NHS
GA
Ocmulgee NM
Andersonville NHS
Jimmy Carter NHS
Chattahoochee River NRA
Carl Sandburg Home NHS
Appalachian NST
Ninety Six NHS
Congaree Swamp NM
SC
Cowpens NB
Kings Mountain NMP
Moores Creek NB
Charles Pinckney NHS
Fort Sumter NM
Fort Pulaski NM
Fort Frederica NM
Cumberland Island NS
Timucuan Ecological and Historical Preserve
Fort Caroline N MEM
Castillo de San Marcos NM
Fort Matanzas NM
FL
Canaveral NS
De Soto N MEM
Big Cypress N PRES
Miami
BISCAYNE NP
EVERGLADES NP
DRY TORTUGAS NP
ATLANTIC OCEAN
NC
Guilford Courthouse NMP
Blue Ridge Pkwy
Wright Brothers N MEM
Fort Raleigh NHS
Cape Hatteras NS
Cape Lookout NS
VA
Booker T. Washington NM
Appomattox Court House NHP
Petersburg NB
Colonial NHP
Maggie L. Walker NHS
Richmond NBP
Fredericksburg and Spotsylvania NMP
Geo. Washington Birthplace NM
Thomas Stone NHS
Assateague Island Natl. Seashore
Manassas NBP
Prince William Forest Park
Washington, D.C.
SHENANDOAH NP
WV
New River Gorge NR
Gauley River NRA
Bluestone NSR
Harpers Ferry NHP
Friendship Hill NHS
Fort Necessity NB
Antietam NB
Catoctin Mtn. Park
Eisenhower NHS
Gettysburg NMP
MD
DE
Allegheny Portage Railroad NHS
Johnstown Flood N MEM
PA
Hopewell Furnace NHS
Valley Forge NHP
Philadelphia
Great Egg Harbor SRR
NJ
Gateway NRA
Morristown NHP
Delaware Water Gap NRA
Steamtown NHS
Upper Delaware SRR
Theodore Roosevelt Inaugural NHS
Women's Rights NHP
Fort Stanwix NM
Saratoga NHP
NY
Martin Van Buren NHS
Vanderbilt Mansion NHS
Home of F.D.R. NHS
Eleanor Roosevelt NHS
New York City
Fire Island NS
Weir Farm NHS
CT
RI
Roger Williams N MEM
MA
Springfield Armory NHS
Boston
Cape Cod NS
VT
NH
Saint-Gaudens NHS
ME
Appalachian NST
St. Croix Island IHS
ACADIA NP
Boston Area
Adams NHS
Boston African American NHS
Boston NHP
F.L. Olmstead NHS
J.F. Kennedy NHS
Longfellow NHS
Lowell NHP
Minute Man NHP
Salem Maritime NHS
Saugus Iron Works NHS
New York City Area
Castle Clinton NM
Edison NHS
Ellis Island NHS
Federal Hall N MEM
General Grant N MEM
Hamilton Grange N MEM
Sagamore Hill NHS
Saint Paul's Church NHS
Statue of Liberty NM
T. Roosevelt Birthplace NHS
Philadelphia Area
Edgar Allen Poe NHS
Independence NHP
T. Kosciuszko N MEM
Baltimore Area
Ft. McHenry NM and Historic Shrine
Hampton NHS
District of Columbia
Constitution Gardens
Ford's Theatre NHS
Franklin Delano Roosevelt Memorial
Frederick Douglass NHS
Korean War Veterans Memorial
Lincoln Memorial
L.B. Johnson Memorial Grove
Mary McLeod Bethune Council House NHS
National Mall
Pennsylvania Avenue NHS
Rock Creek Park
T. Roosevelt Island
Thomas Jefferson Memorial
Vietnam Veterans Memorial
Washington Monument
White House
Maryland
Chesapeake and Ohio Canal NHP
Clara Barton NHS
Fort Washington Park
Greenbelt Park
Monocacy NB
Piscataway Park
Potomac Heritage NST
Virginia
Arlington House
George Washington Memorial Parkway
Wolf Trap Farm Park for the Performing Arts
National Park System
National Parks
Other Parks
0 100 200 300 400 500 mi
0 100 200 300 400 500 km
PUERTO RICO
San Juan NHS
ATLANTIC OCEAN
VIRGIN ISLANDS NP
VIRGIN ISLANDS
Buck Island Reef NM
Christiansted NHS
Salt River Bay NHP and Ecological Preserve
Caribbean Sea
0 100 200 miles
0 100 200 km
© GeoSystems Global Corp.

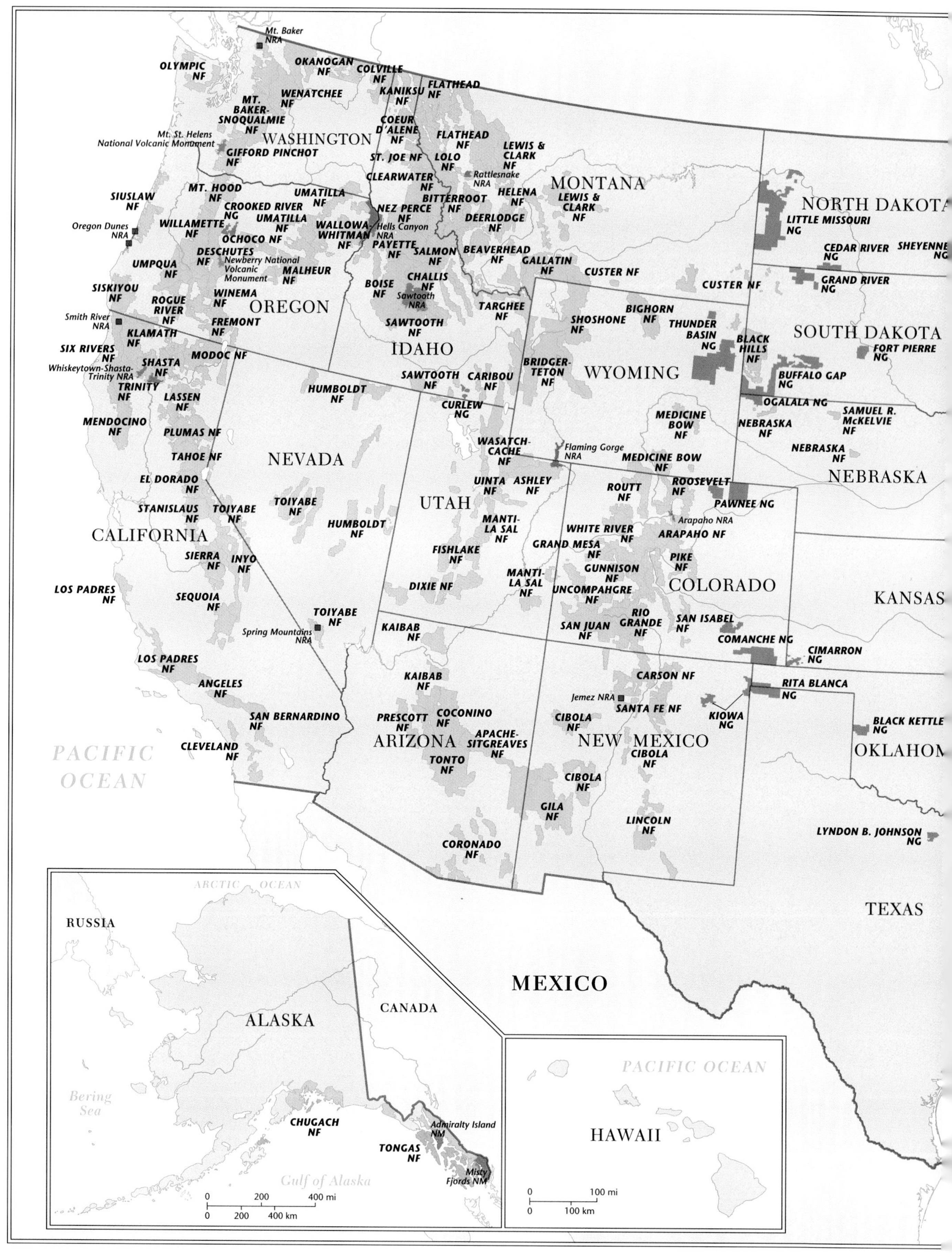
Mt. Baker NRA
OLYMPIC NF
OKANOGAN NF
COLVILLE NF
KANIKSU NF
FLATHEAD NF
WENATCHEE NF
MT. BAKER-SNOQUALMIE NF
COEUR D'ALENE NF
Mt. St. Helens National Volcanic Monument
WASHINGTON
FLATHEAD NF
LEWIS & CLARK NF
GIFFORD PINCHOT NF
ST. JOE NF
LOLO NF
Rattlesnake NRA
CLEARWATER NF
MONTANA
SIUSLAW NF
MT. HOOD NF
UMATILLA NF
BITTERROOT NF
HELENA NF
LEWIS & CLARK NF
NORTH DAKOTA
CROOKED RIVER NG
NEZ PERCE NF
Oregon Dunes NRA
WILLAMETTE NF
UMATILLA NF
WALLOWA-WHITMAN NF
Hells Canyon NRA
DEERLODGE NF
LITTLE MISSOURI NG
OCHOCO NF
PAYETTE NF
BEAVERHEAD NF
CEDAR RIVER NG
SHEYENNE NG
DESCHUTES NF
Newberry National Volcanic Monument
SALMON NF
GALLATIN NF
UMPQUA NF
MALHEUR NF
CUSTER NF
CHALLIS NF
GRAND RIVER NG
SISKIYOU NF
WINEMA NF
BOISE NF
Sawtooth NRA
CUSTER NF
ROGUE RIVER NF
OREGON
TARGHEE NF
BIGHORN NF
Smith River NRA
FREMONT NF
SHOSHONE NF
THUNDER BASIN NG
KLAMATH NF
SAWTOOTH NF
SOUTH DAKOTA
BLACK HILLS NF
SIX RIVERS NF
MODOC NF
IDAHO
FORT PIERRE NG
Whiskeytown-Shasta-Trinity NRA
SHASTA NF
BRIDGER-TETON NF
WYOMING
SAWTOOTH NF
CARIBOU NF
BUFFALO GAP NG
TRINITY NF
HUMBOLDT NF
LASSEN NF
CURLEW NG
OGALALA NG
SAMUEL R. McKELVIE NF
MENDOCINO NF
MEDICINE BOW NF
NEBRASKA NF
PLUMAS NF
WASATCH-CACHE NF
Flaming Gorge NRA
NEBRASKA NF
TAHOE NF
NEVADA
MEDICINE BOW NF
NEBRASKA
EL DORADO NF
UINTA NF
ASHLEY NF
ROUTT NF
ROOSEVELT NF
TOIYABE NF
PAWNEE NG
STANISLAUS NF
TOIYABE NF
UTAH
Arapaho NRA
HUMBOLDT NF
MANTI-LA SAL NF
WHITE RIVER NF
ARAPAHO NF
CALIFORNIA
GRAND MESA NF
FISHLAKE NF
PIKE NF
SIERRA NF
INYO NF
GUNNISON NF
MANTI-LA SAL NF
COLORADO
LOS PADRES NF
DIXIE NF
UNCOMPAHGRE NF
KANSAS
SEQUOIA NF
RIO GRANDE NF
TOIYABE NF
KAIBAB NF
SAN ISABEL NF
Spring Mountains NRA
SAN JUAN NF
COMANCHE NG
CIMARRON NG
LOS PADRES NF
KAIBAB NF
CARSON NF
ANGELES NF
RITA BLANCA NG
Jemez NRA
SANTA FE NF
SAN BERNARDINO NF
PRESCOTT NF
COCONINO NF
CIBOLA NF
KIOWA NG
BLACK KETTLE NG
APACHE-SITGREAVES NF
ARIZONA
NEW MEXICO
PACIFIC OCEAN
CLEVELAND NF
OKLAHOMA
CIBOLA NF
TONTO NF
CIBOLA NF
GILA NF
LINCOLN NF
LYNDON B. JOHNSON NG
CORONADO NF
TEXAS
MEXICO
ARCTIC OCEAN
RUSSIA
CANADA
ALASKA
Bering Sea
CHUGACH NF
Admiralty Island NM
TONGAS NF
Misty Fjords NM
Gulf of Alaska
0 200 400 mi
0 200 400 km
PACIFIC OCEAN
HAWAII
0 100 mi
0 100 km

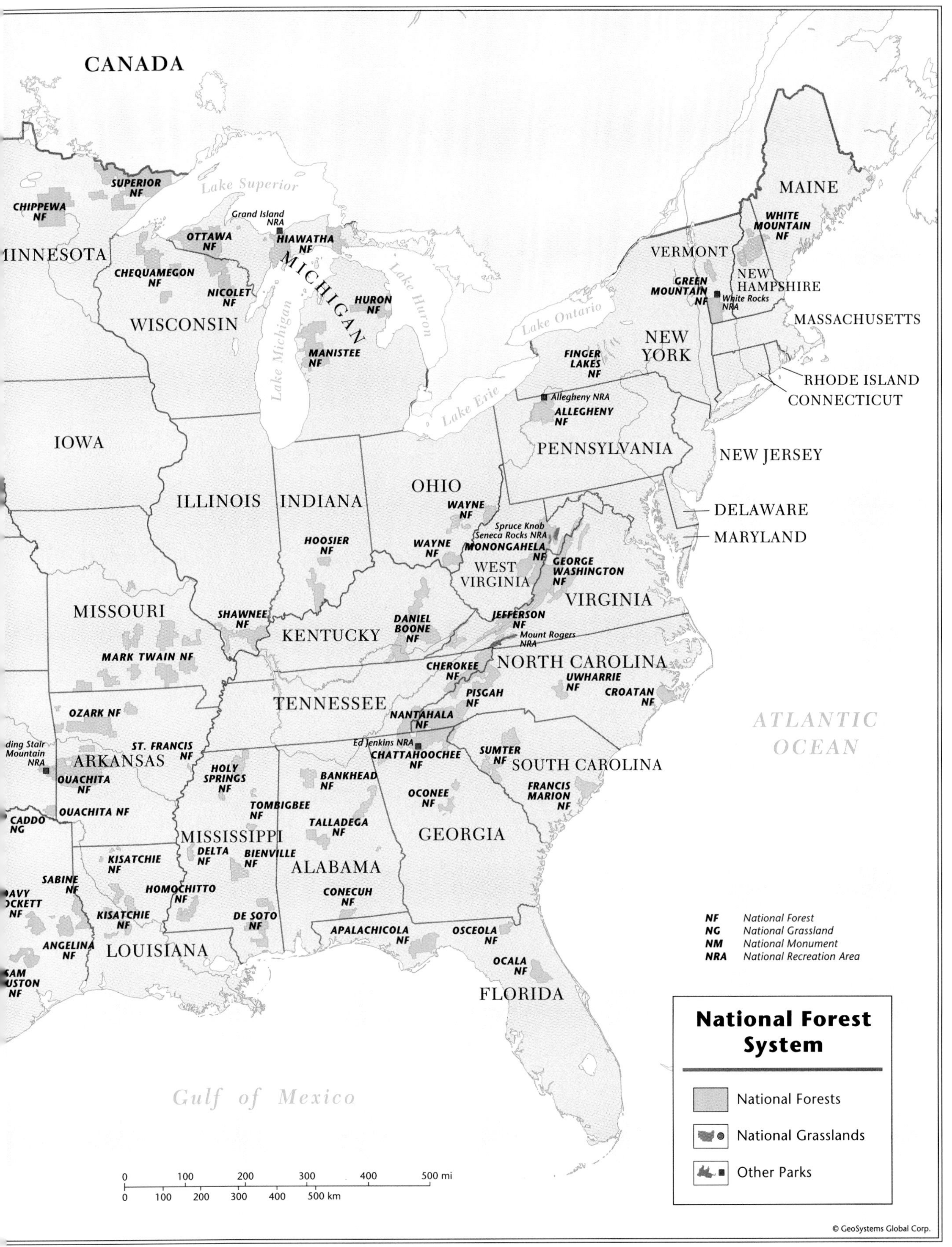

CANADA
Lake Superior
Lake Michigan
Lake Huron
Lake Ontario
Lake Erie
SUPERIOR NF
CHIPPEWA NF
MINNESOTA
Grand Island NRA
OTTAWA NF
HIAWATHA NF
MICHIGAN
CHEQUAMEGON NF
NICOLET NF
HURON NF
WISCONSIN
MANISTEE NF
MAINE
WHITE MOUNTAIN NF
VERMONT
GREEN MOUNTAIN NF
NEW HAMPSHIRE
White Rocks NRA
MASSACHUSETTS
NEW YORK
FINGER LAKES NF
RHODE ISLAND
CONNECTICUT
Allegheny NRA
ALLEGHENY NF
PENNSYLVANIA
NEW JERSEY
IOWA
ILLINOIS
INDIANA
OHIO
WAYNE NF
DELAWARE
MARYLAND
Spruce Knob Seneca Rocks NRA
HOOSIER NF
WAYNE NF
MONONGAHELA NF
WEST VIRGINIA
GEORGE WASHINGTON NF
VIRGINIA
MISSOURI
SHAWNEE NF
DANIEL BOONE NF
KENTUCKY
JEFFERSON NF
Mount Rogers NRA
MARK TWAIN NF
CHEROKEE NF
NORTH CAROLINA
UWHARRIE NF
CROATAN NF
PISGAH NF
TENNESSEE
OZARK NF
NANTAHALA NF
ATLANTIC OCEAN
ST. FRANCIS NF
Ed Jenkins NRA
CHATTAHOOCHEE NF
SUMTER NF
SOUTH CAROLINA
ARKANSAS
OUACHITA NF
HOLY SPRINGS NF
BANKHEAD NF
OCONEE NF
FRANCIS MARION NF
OUACHITA NF
TOMBIGBEE NF
CADDO NG
TALLADEGA NF
GEORGIA
MISSISSIPPI
DELTA NF
BIENVILLE NF
KISATCHIE NF
ALABAMA
SABINE NF
HOMOCHITTO NF
CONECUH NF
KISATCHIE NF
DE SOTO NF
APALACHICOLA NF
OSCEOLA NF
ANGELINA NF
LOUISIANA
OCALA NF
FLORIDA
Gulf of Mexico
NF National Forest
NG National Grassland
NM National Monument
NRA National Recreation Area
National Forest System
National Forests
National Grasslands
Other Parks
0 100 200 300 400 500 mi
0 100 200 300 400 500 km
© GeoSystems Global Corp.

# National Wildlife Refuges

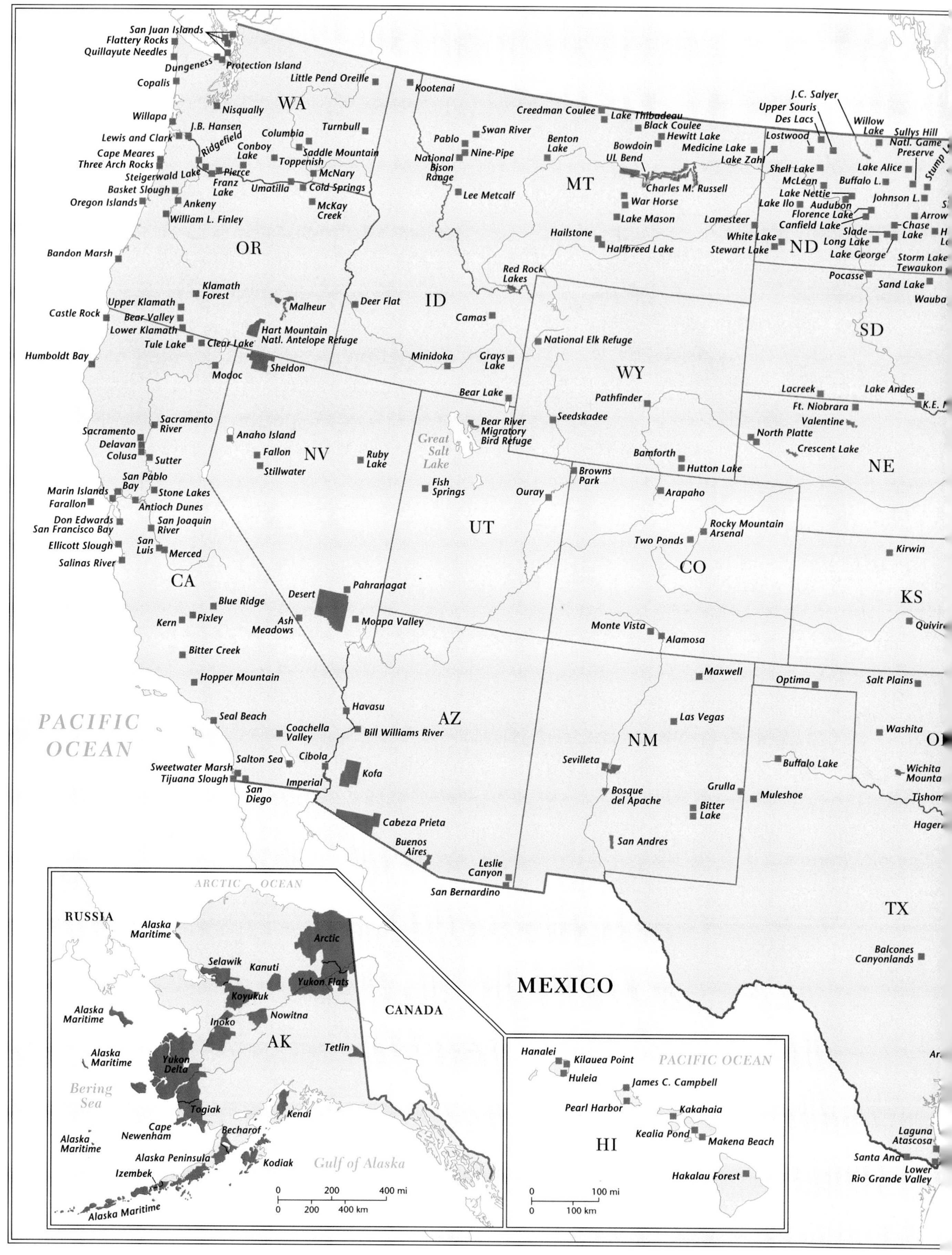
WA
OR
ID
MT
ND
SD
WY
NE
NV
UT
CO
CA
KS
AZ
NM
TX
PACIFIC OCEAN
MEXICO
Great Salt Lake
San Juan Islands
Flattery Rocks
Quillayute Needles
Dungeness
Protection Island
Copalis
Little Pend Oreille
Kootenai
Nisqually
Willapa
J.B. Hansen
Lewis and Clark
Ridgefield
Columbia
Turnbull
Conboy Lake
Saddle Mountain
Toppenish
Cape Meares
Three Arch Rocks
Steigerwald Lake
Pierce
Franz Lake
McNary
Basket Slough
Umatilla
Cold Springs
Oregon Islands
Ankeny
McKay Creek
William L. Finley
Bandon Marsh
Klamath Forest
Upper Klamath
Malheur
Deer Flat
Castle Rock
Bear Valley
Lower Klamath
Hart Mountain Natl. Antelope Refuge
Tule Lake
Clear Lake
Humboldt Bay
Sheldon
Modoc
Pablo
Swan River
National Bison Range
Nine-Pipe
Lee Metcalf
Camas
Minidoka
Grays Lake
Bear Lake
Creedman Coulee
Lake Thibadeau
Black Coulee
Hewitt Lake
Benton Lake
Bowdoin
Medicine Lake
UL Bend
Charles M. Russell
War Horse
Lake Mason
Hailstone
Halfbreed Lake
Red Rock Lakes
Lamesteer
J.C. Salyer
Upper Souris
Des Lacs
Willow Lake
Sullys Hill Natl. Game Preserve
Lostwood
Lake Zahl
Shell Lake
Lake Alice
McLean
Buffalo L.
Stump L
Lake Nettie
Johnson L.
Lake Ilo
Audubon
Florence Lake
Arrow
Canfield Lake
Chase Lake
White Lake
Slade
Long Lake
Stewart Lake
Lake George
Storm Lake
Tewaukon
Pocasse
Sand Lake
Wauba
National Elk Refuge
Lacreek
Lake Andes
K.E.
Ft. Niobrara
Valentine
North Platte
Crescent Lake
Pathfinder
Seedskadee
Bear River Migratory Bird Refuge
Bamforth
Hutton Lake
Browns Park
Ouray
Fish Springs
Arapaho
Rocky Mountain Arsenal
Two Ponds
Kirwin
Quivir
Sacramento
Sacramento River
Delavan
Colusa
Sutter
Anaho Island
Fallon
Stillwater
Ruby Lake
San Pablo Bay
Marin Islands
Farallon
Stone Lakes
Antioch Dunes
Don Edwards San Francisco Bay
San Joaquin River
Ellicott Slough
San Luis
Merced
Salinas River
Desert
Pahranagat
Blue Ridge
Kern
Pixley
Ash Meadows
Moapa Valley
Bitter Creek
Hopper Mountain
Monte Vista
Alamosa
Maxwell
Optima
Salt Plains
Havasu
Seal Beach
Coachella Valley
Bill Williams River
Las Vegas
Washita
Salton Sea
Cibola
Sweetwater Marsh
Tijuana Slough
Kofa
Sevilleta
Buffalo Lake
Wichita Mounta
Imperial
San Diego
Bosque del Apache
Grulla
Muleshoe
Tishom
Bitter Lake
Cabeza Prieta
Hager
San Andres
Buenos Aires
Leslie Canyon
San Bernardino
Balcones Canyonlands
Laguna Atascosa
Santa Ana
Lower Rio Grande Valley
ARCTIC OCEAN
RUSSIA
Alaska Maritime
Arctic
Selawik
Kanuti
Yukon Flats
Koyukuk
CANADA
Nowitna
Innoko
AK
Tetlin
Yukon Delta
Bering Sea
Togiak
Kenai
Cape Newenham
Becharof
Alaska Peninsula
Kodiak
Gulf of Alaska
Izembek
0 200 400 mi
0 200 400 km
Hanalei
Kilauea Point
PACIFIC OCEAN
Huleia
James C. Campbell
Pearl Harbor
Kakahaia
Kealia Pond
Makena Beach
HI
Hakalau Forest
0 100 mi
0 100 km

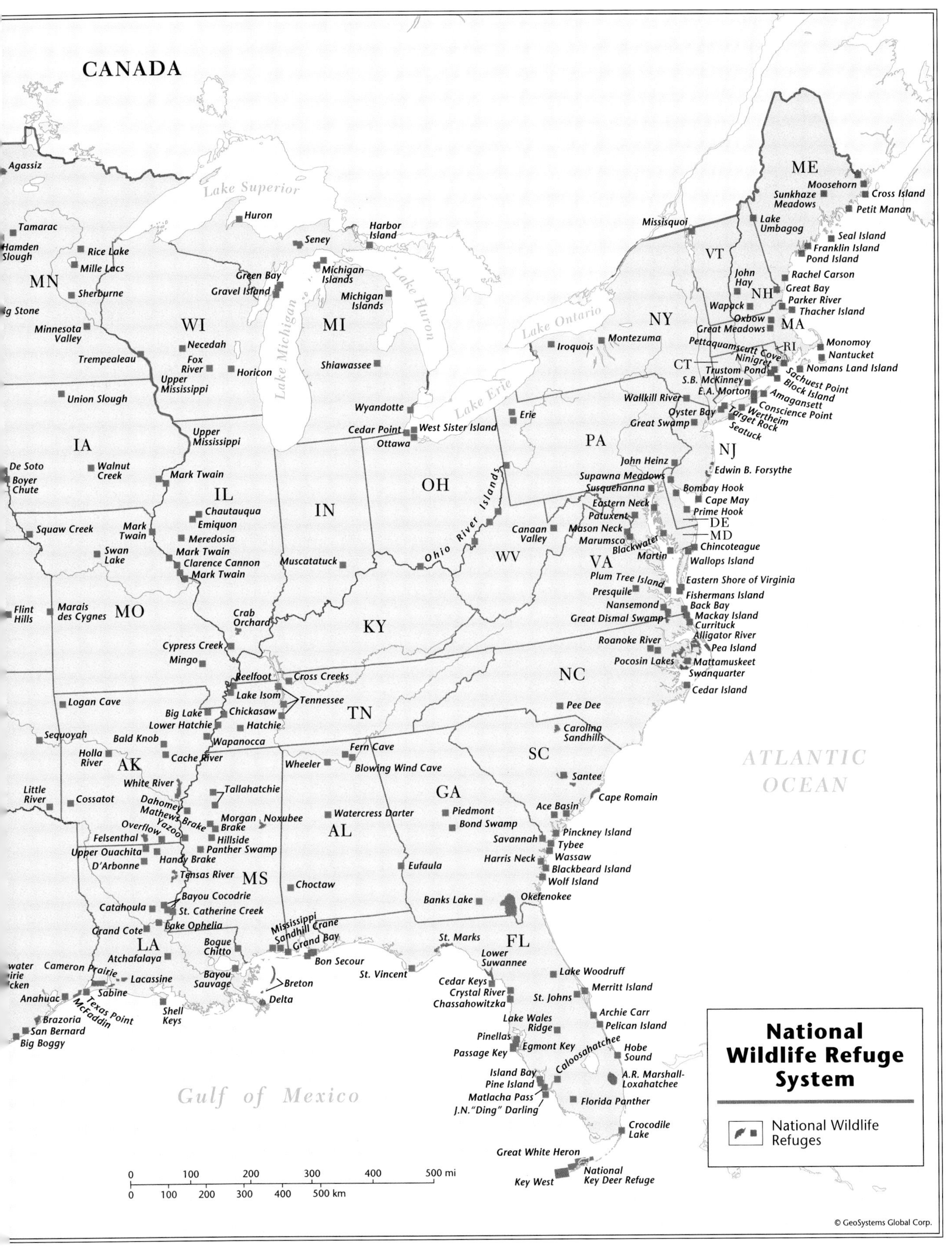

CANADA
Lake Superior
Lake Michigan
Lake Huron
Lake Ontario
Lake Erie
ATLANTIC OCEAN
Gulf of Mexico
ME
Moosehorn
Cross Island
Sunkhaze Meadows
Petit Manan
Lake Umbagog
Missisquoi
Seal Island
Franklin Island
Pond Island
VT
John Hay
NH
Rachel Carson
Great Bay
Parker River
Thacher Island
Wapack
Oxbow
Great Meadows
MA
NY
Montezuma
Iroquois
Monomoy
Nantucket
Pettaquamscutt Cove
RI
Ninigret
Nomans Land Island
CT
Trustom Pond
S.B. McKinney
Sachuest Point
Block Island
E.A. Morton
Amagansett
Conscience Point
Wertheim
Target Rock
Seatuck
Wallkill River
Oyster Bay
Great Swamp
Agassiz
Tamarac
Hamden Slough
Rice Lake
Mille Lacs
MN
Sherburne
Big Stone
Minnesota Valley
Trempealeau
Huron
Seney
Harbor Island
Michigan Islands
Green Bay
Gravel Island
WI
MI
Necedah
Fox River
Horicon
Upper Mississippi
Shiawassee
Union Slough
Wyandotte
Erie
Cedar Point
West Sister Island
Ottawa
PA
IA
Upper Mississippi
De Soto
Boyer Chute
Walnut Creek
Mark Twain
IL
Chautauqua
Emiquon
IN
OH
John Heinz
NJ
Edwin B. Forsythe
Supawna Meadows
Susquehanna
Bombay Hook
Cape May
Eastern Neck
Prime Hook
DE
Patuxent
Mason Neck
Canaan Valley
MD
Marumsco
Blackwater
Chincoteague
Martin
Wallops Island
WV
VA
Ohio River Islands
Squaw Creek
Mark Twain
Meredosia
Swan Lake
Mark Twain
Clarence Cannon
Mark Twain
Muscatatuck
Plum Tree Island
Eastern Shore of Virginia
Presquile
Fishermans Island
Nansemond
Back Bay
Great Dismal Swamp
Mackay Island
Currituck
Alligator River
Pea Island
Flint Hills
Marais des Cygnes
MO
Crab Orchard
KY
Cypress Creek
Mingo
Roanoke River
Pocosin Lakes
Mattamuskeet
Swanquarter
Cedar Island
Reelfoot
Cross Creeks
NC
Lake Isom
Tennessee
Logan Cave
Big Lake
Chickasaw
TN
Pee Dee
Lower Hatchie
Hatchie
Carolina Sandhills
Sequoyah
Bald Knob
Wapanocca
Holla Bend River
Cache River
AK
Fern Cave
SC
Wheeler
Blowing Wind Cave
Santee
White River
Little River
Cossatot
Tallahatchie
Cape Romain
GA
Dahomey
Mathews Brake
Yazoo
Morgan Brake
Noxubee
Watercress Darter
Piedmont
Ace Basin
Overflow
Felsenthal
Hillside
AL
Bond Swamp
Pinckney Island
Upper Ouachita
Panther Swamp
Savannah
Tybee
D'Arbonne
Handy Brake
Harris Neck
Wassaw
Tensas River
MS
Eufaula
Blackbeard Island
Wolf Island
Choctaw
Bayou Cocodrie
Catahoula
St. Catherine Creek
Banks Lake
Okefenokee
Grand Cote
Lake Ophelia
Mississippi Sandhill Crane
LA
Bogue Chitto
Grand Bay
St. Marks
FL
Atchafalaya
Bon Secour
Lower Suwannee
Lake Woodruff
Cameron Prairie
Lacassine
St. Vincent
Bayou Sauvage
Breton
Cedar Keys
Merritt Island
Sabine
Crystal River
St. Johns
Anahuac
Delta
Chassahowitzka
Texas Point
Shell Keys
Archie Carr
McFaddin
Lake Wales Ridge
Pelican Island
Brazoria
San Bernard
Pinellas
Caloosahatchee
Big Boggy
Egmont Key
Hobe Sound
Passage Key
Island Bay
A.R. Marshall-Loxahatchee
Pine Island
Matlacha Pass
Florida Panther
J.N. "Ding" Darling
Crocodile Lake
Great White Heron
Key West
National Key Deer Refuge
0 100 200 300 400 500 mi
0 100 200 300 400 500 km
National Wildlife Refuge System
National Wildlife Refuges
© GeoSystems Global Corp.

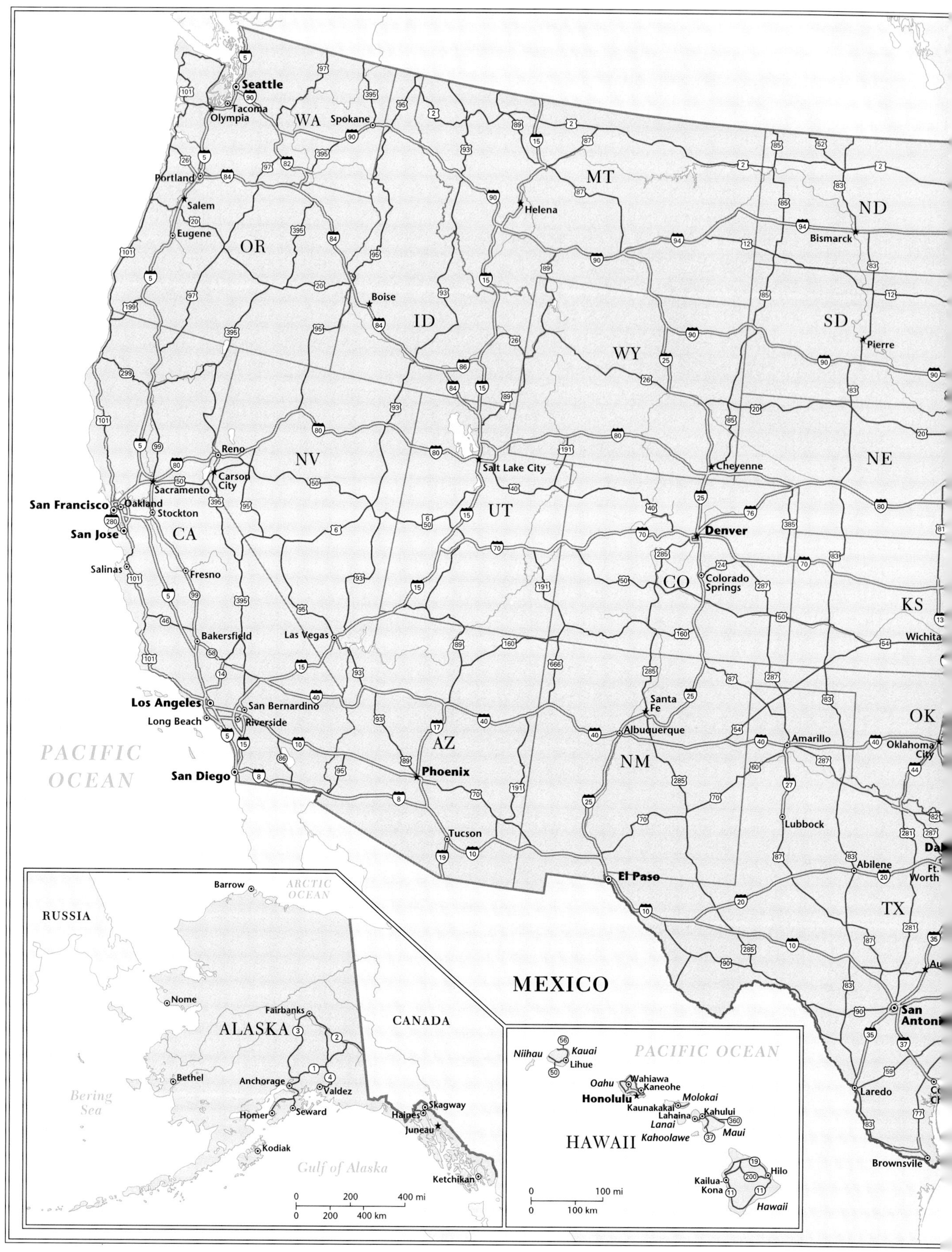
WA
Seattle
Tacoma
Olympia
Spokane
Portland
Salem
Eugene
OR
Boise
ID
MT
Helena
ND
Bismarck
SD
Pierre
WY
Cheyenne
NE
Reno
Carson City
NV
Salt Lake City
UT
Sacramento
San Francisco
Oakland
Stockton
San Jose
CA
Salinas
Fresno
Denver
CO
Colorado Springs
KS
Wichita
Bakersfield
Las Vegas
Los Angeles
San Bernardino
Long Beach
Riverside
San Diego
PACIFIC OCEAN
AZ
Phoenix
Tucson
Santa Fe
Albuquerque
NM
OK
Amarillo
Oklahoma City
Lubbock
El Paso
Abilene
Ft. Worth
TX
MEXICO
San Antonio
Laredo
Brownsvile
Barrow
ARCTIC OCEAN
RUSSIA
Nome
ALASKA
Fairbanks
CANADA
Bethel
Anchorage
Valdez
Bering Sea
Homer
Seward
Skagway
Haines
Juneau
Kodiak
Gulf of Alaska
Ketchikan
0 200 400 mi
0 200 400 km
Niihau
Kauai
Lihue
PACIFIC OCEAN
Oahu
Wahiawa
Kaneohe
Honolulu
Molokai
Kaunakakai
Lahaina
Kahului
Lanai
Maui
HAWAII
Kahoolawe
Hilo
Kailua-Kona
Hawaii
0 100 mi
0 100 km

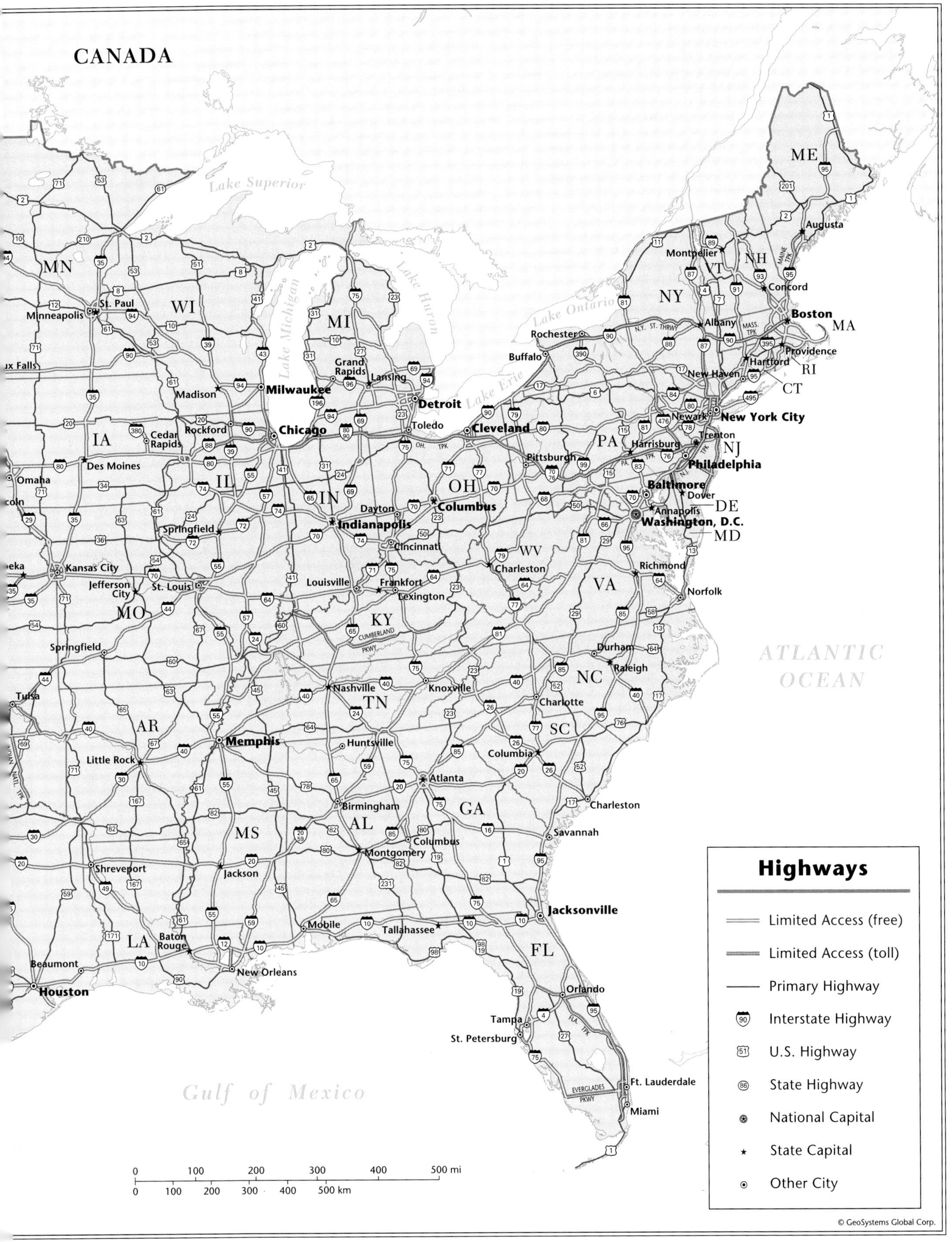
CANADA
Lake Superior
Lake Michigan
Lake Huron
Lake Ontario
Lake Erie
ATLANTIC OCEAN
Gulf of Mexico
MN
WI
MI
IA
IL
IN
OH
PA
NY
VT
NH
ME
MA
RI
CT
NJ
DE
MD
VA
WV
KY
MO
TN
NC
SC
GA
AL
MS
AR
LA
FL
St. Paul
Minneapolis
Madison
Milwaukee
Chicago
Rockford
Cedar Rapids
Des Moines
Omaha
Kansas City
Jefferson City
St. Louis
Springfield
Indianapolis
Dayton
Columbus
Cincinnati
Louisville
Frankfort
Lexington
Charleston
Richmond
Norfolk
Washington, D.C.
Annapolis
Dover
Baltimore
Philadelphia
Trenton
Harrisburg
Pittsburgh
Cleveland
Toledo
Detroit
Lansing
Grand Rapids
Buffalo
Rochester
Albany
Montpelier
Concord
Augusta
Boston
Providence
Hartford
New Haven
Newark
New York City
Nashville
Knoxville
Durham
Raleigh
Charlotte
Columbia
Charleston
Savannah
Atlanta
Huntsville
Birmingham
Montgomery
Columbus
Memphis
Little Rock
Tulsa
Shreveport
Jackson
Mobile
Tallahassee
Jacksonville
Baton Rouge
New Orleans
Beaumont
Houston
Orlando
Tampa
St. Petersburg
Ft. Lauderdale
Miami
N.Y. ST. THRWY
MASS. TPK
MAINE TPK
OH. TPK
PA. TPK
CUMBERLAND PKWY
FLA. TPK
EVERGLADES PKWY
Highways
Limited Access (free)
Limited Access (toll)
Primary Highway
Interstate Highway
U.S. Highway
State Highway
National Capital
State Capital
Other City
0 100 200 300 400 500 mi
0 100 200 300 400 500 km
© GeoSystems Global Corp.

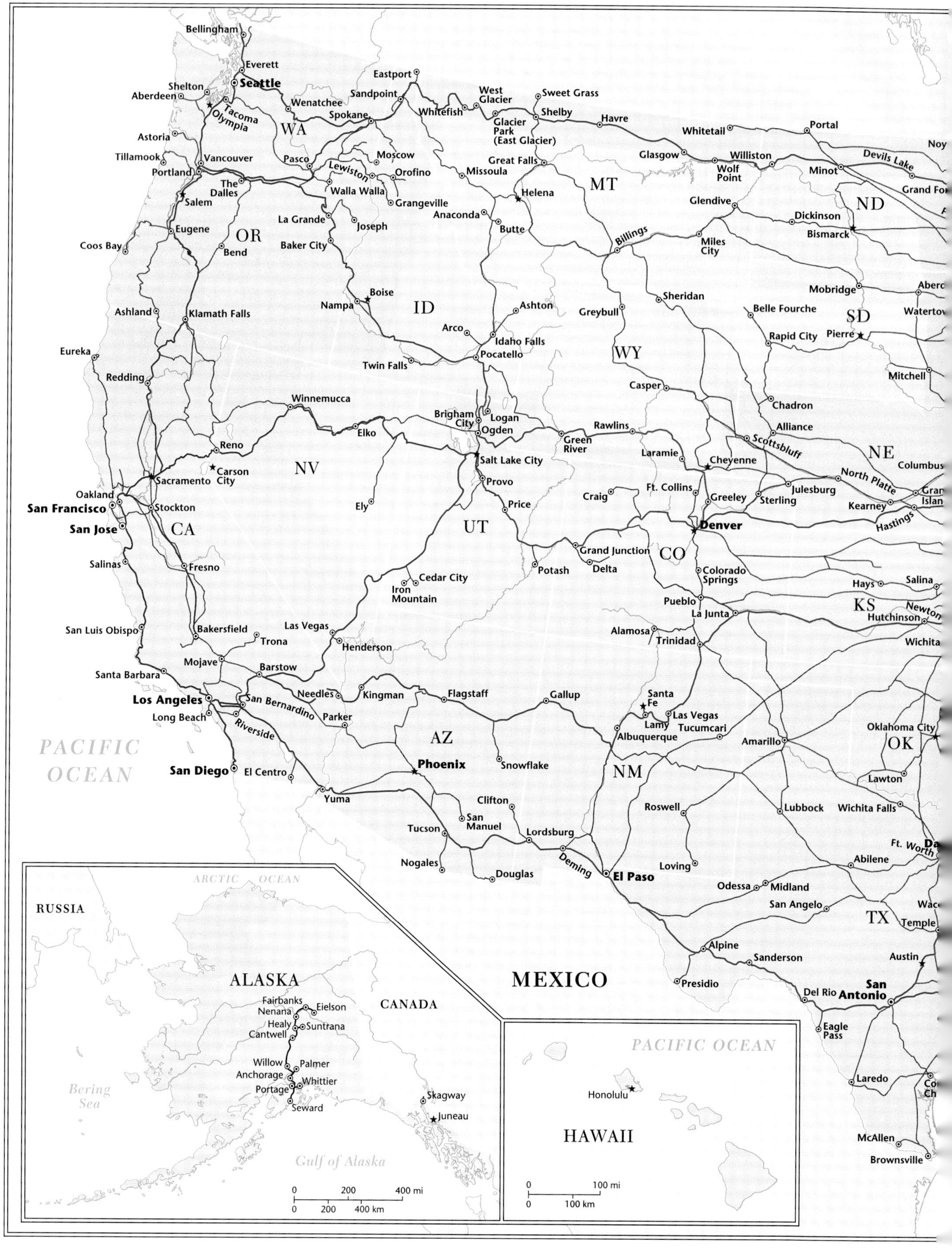
PACIFIC OCEAN
MEXICO
WA
OR
CA
NV
ID
MT
WY
UT
AZ
CO
NM
ND
SD
NE
KS
OK
TX
Bellingham
Everett
Seattle
Shelton
Aberdeen
Tacoma
Olympia
Wenatchee
Spokane
Sandpoint
Eastport
Whitefish
West Glacier
Glacier Park (East Glacier)
Sweet Grass
Shelby
Havre
Whitetail
Portal
Astoria
Tillamook
Vancouver
Portland
Pasco
Moscow
Lewiston
Orofino
Walla Walla
Grangeville
The Dalles
Salem
Eugene
Coos Bay
Bend
La Grande
Joseph
Baker City
Great Falls
Missoula
Helena
Anaconda
Butte
Glasgow
Williston
Wolf Point
Minot
Devils Lake
Glendive
Dickinson
Bismarck
Billings
Miles City
Boise
Nampa
Ashland
Klamath Falls
Eureka
Redding
Ashton
Arco
Idaho Falls
Pocatello
Twin Falls
Greybull
Sheridan
Mobridge
Belle Fourche
Rapid City
Pierre
Casper
Mitchell
Chadron
Alliance
Scottsbluff
Winnemucca
Elko
Reno
Brigham City
Logan
Ogden
Rawlins
Green River
Laramie
Cheyenne
Salt Lake City
Sacramento
Carson City
Oakland
San Francisco
San Jose
Stockton
Provo
Price
Ely
Craig
Ft. Collins
Greeley
Sterling
Julesburg
North Platte
Kearney
Hastings
Denver
Grand Junction
Delta
Potash
Salinas
Fresno
Cedar City
Iron Mountain
Colorado Springs
Pueblo
La Junta
Hays
Salina
Newton
Hutchinson
Wichita
San Luis Obispo
Bakersfield
Las Vegas
Trona
Henderson
Alamosa
Trinidad
Mojave
Santa Barbara
Barstow
Los Angeles
Long Beach
Needles
San Bernardino
Kingman
Parker
Riverside
Flagstaff
Gallup
Santa Fe
Lamy
Las Vegas
Albuquerque
Tucumcari
Amarillo
Oklahoma City
Lawton
San Diego
El Centro
Phoenix
Snowflake
Yuma
Clifton
San Manuel
Tucson
Nogales
Douglas
Lordsburg
Deming
El Paso
Roswell
Loving
Lubbock
Wichita Falls
Ft. Worth
Abilene
Odessa
Midland
San Angelo
Temple
Alpine
Sanderson
Austin
Presidio
Del Rio
San Antonio
Eagle Pass
Laredo
McAllen
Brownsville
Columbus
Noy
Grand Fo
Aberd
Waterto
Gran Islan
Da
Wac
ARCTIC OCEAN
RUSSIA
ALASKA
CANADA
Bering Sea
Gulf of Alaska
Fairbanks
Eielson
Nenana
Healy
Suntrana
Cantwell
Willow
Palmer
Anchorage
Whittier
Portage
Seward
Skagway
Juneau
0 200 400 mi
0 200 400 km
PACIFIC OCEAN
Honolulu
HAWAII
0 100 mi
0 100 km

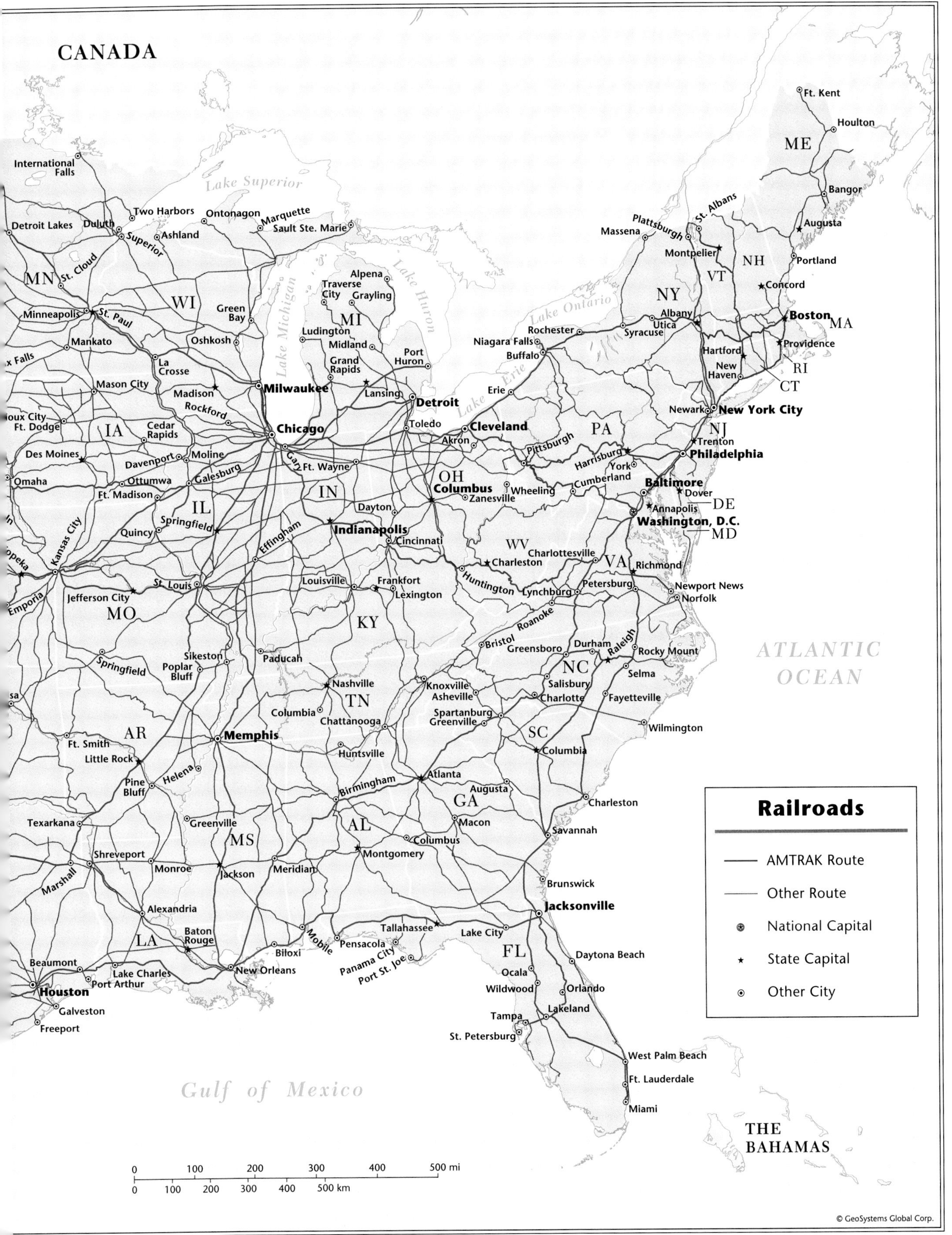
CANADA
Lake Superior
Lake Michigan
Lake Huron
Lake Ontario
Lake Erie
ATLANTIC OCEAN
Gulf of Mexico
THE BAHAMAS
Railroads
AMTRAK Route
Other Route
National Capital
State Capital
Other City
0 100 200 300 400 500 mi
0 100 200 300 400 500 km
ME
NH
VT
NY
MA
RI
CT
NJ
PA
DE
MD
VA
WV
NC
SC
GA
FL
AL
MS
TN
KY
OH
IN
IL
MI
WI
MN
IA
MO
AR
LA
Ft. Kent
Houlton
Bangor
Augusta
Portland
Concord
Boston
Providence
Hartford
New Haven
New York City
Newark
Trenton
Philadelphia
Dover
Baltimore
Annapolis
Washington, D.C.
Richmond
Newport News
Norfolk
Petersburg
Lynchburg
Charlottesville
Roanoke
Bristol
Greensboro
Durham
Raleigh
Rocky Mount
Selma
Salisbury
Charlotte
Fayetteville
Wilmington
Columbia
Charleston
Savannah
Brunswick
Jacksonville
Lake City
Tallahassee
Daytona Beach
Ocala
Wildwood
Orlando
Lakeland
Tampa
St. Petersburg
West Palm Beach
Ft. Lauderdale
Miami
St. Albans
Plattsburgh
Massena
Montpelier
Albany
Utica
Syracuse
Rochester
Niagara Falls
Buffalo
Erie
Pittsburgh
Harrisburg
York
Cumberland
Wheeling
Cleveland
Akron
Toledo
Detroit
Port Huron
Lansing
Grand Rapids
Midland
Ludington
Traverse City
Grayling
Alpena
Columbus
Zanesville
Dayton
Cincinnati
Indianapolis
Ft. Wayne
Gary
Chicago
Milwaukee
Madison
Rockford
Oshkosh
Green Bay
La Crosse
Ashland
Ontonagon
Marquette
Sault Ste. Marie
Two Harbors
Duluth
Superior
Detroit Lakes
International Falls
St. Cloud
Minneapolis
St. Paul
Mankato
Sioux Falls
Mason City
Sioux City
Ft. Dodge
Cedar Rapids
Des Moines
Davenport
Moline
Omaha
Ottumwa
Galesburg
Ft. Madison
Quincy
Springfield
Effingham
Kansas City
Topeka
Emporia
Jefferson City
St. Louis
Louisville
Frankfort
Lexington
Charleston
Huntington
Springfield
Sikeston
Poplar Bluff
Paducah
Nashville
Columbia
Chattanooga
Knoxville
Asheville
Spartanburg
Greenville
Huntsville
Memphis
Ft. Smith
Little Rock
Helena
Pine Bluff
Texarkana
Atlanta
Augusta
Macon
Birmingham
Columbus
Montgomery
Greenville
Shreveport
Monroe
Jackson
Meridian
Marshall
Alexandria
Baton Rouge
Mobile
Pensacola
Panama City
Port St. Joe
Biloxi
New Orleans
Beaumont
Lake Charles
Port Arthur
Houston
Galveston
Freeport
© GeoSystems Global Corp.

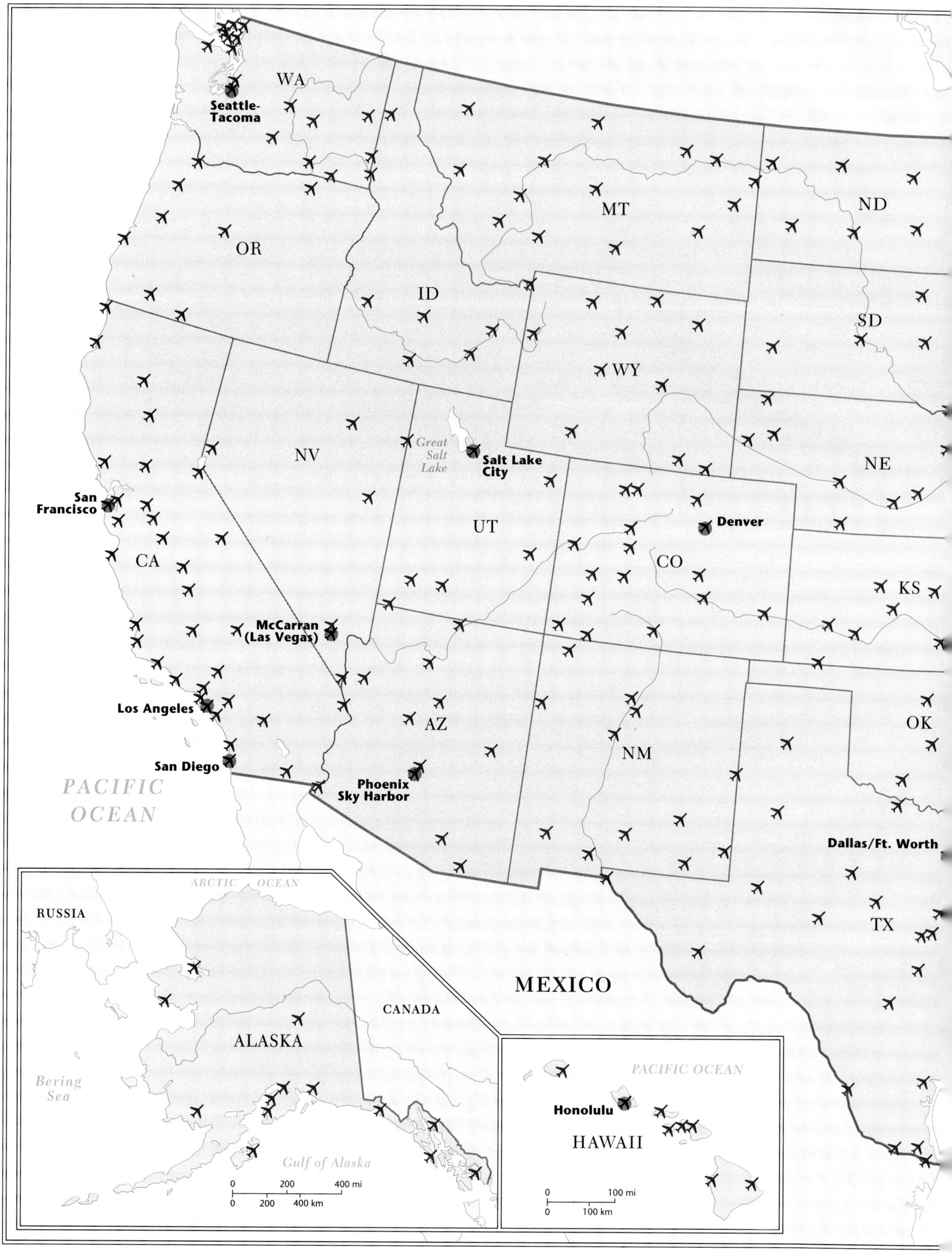
WA
Seattle-Tacoma
OR
MT
ND
ID
SD
WY
NV
Great Salt Lake
Salt Lake City
NE
San Francisco
UT
Denver
CA
CO
KS
McCarran (Las Vegas)
Los Angeles
AZ
OK
NM
San Diego
Phoenix Sky Harbor
PACIFIC OCEAN
Dallas/Ft. Worth
TX
MEXICO
ARCTIC OCEAN
RUSSIA
CANADA
ALASKA
Bering Sea
Gulf of Alaska
0 200 400 mi
0 200 400 km
PACIFIC OCEAN
Honolulu
HAWAII
0 100 mi
0 100 km

CANADA
Lake Superior
Lake Michigan
Lake Huron
Lake Ontario
Lake Erie
ATLANTIC OCEAN
Gulf of Mexico
THE BAHAMAS
MN
WI
MI
IA
IL
IN
OH
PA
NY
VT
NH
ME
MA
CT
RI
NJ
DE
MD
WV
VA
KY
MO
TN
NC
SC
GA
AL
MS
AR
LA
FL
Minneapolis-St. Paul
Chicago O'Hare
Detroit Metropolitan Wayne County
Cleveland-Hopkins
Pittsburgh
La Guardia (NYC)
John F. Kennedy (NYC)
Newark
Logan (Boston)
Philadelphia
Baltimore-Washington
Washington National
Washington-Dulles
Cincinnati/Northern Kentucky
Lambert-St. Louis
Charlotte/Douglas
Hartsfield Atlanta
Houston Intercontinental
Orlando
Tampa
Ft. Lauderdale/Hollywood
Miami
Commercial Airports
Busiest Airports (in terms of passenger arrivals and departures)
Other Commercial Airports
0 100 200 300 400 500 mi
0 100 200 300 400 500 km
© GeoSystems Global Corp.

# *MapSkills*™

Maps are tools that provide us with information about the world in which we live. As with all tools, we need skills in order to use them well. With these skills we can use maps to:

- find the **location** of places on Earth
- see the **distribution** of natural and human-made elements of our world
- make comparisons to discover **relationships** among places, people, or things

The information on the following pages will help you get the most from the many maps in *Maps of the World.*

## *Contents*

# Understanding Maps

Maps are special pictures of places on Earth. For thousands of years human beings have drawn maps—on clay tablets and in stone, on paper and in the sand. All of these maps are alike in important ways:

- All maps are a view from above
- All maps show selected information using symbols
- All maps are smaller than the real place on Earth that they show

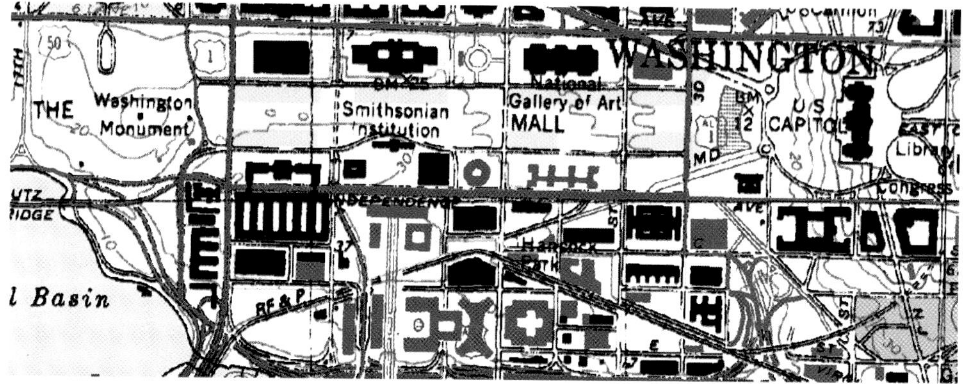


*This map shows part of Washington, D.C.—the Mall from the Washington Monument to the United States Capitol. You can imagine that you are a bird looking directly down at the area.*

*Compared to this photograph of Washington, the map above shows only some of the buildings and streets that are there. The mapmaker, or cartographer, has selected the information important for the purpose of this map. The map uses symbols and words to show you that information.*

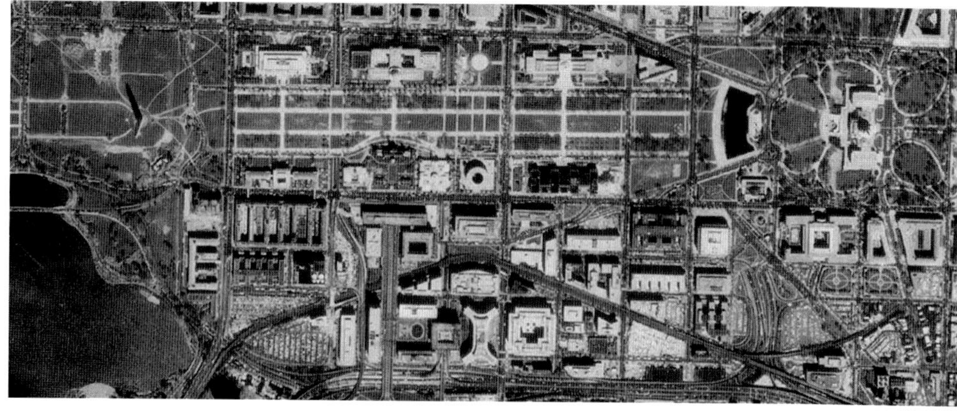

# Different Kinds of Maps

Because people want to show many different things on Earth, they create many different kinds of maps.

## Physical Maps

The purpose of a **physical map** is to show the physical or natural world. Physical maps show landforms and bodies of water. We use physical maps to locate rivers and mountains, ocean currents and wind patterns. See Volumes 3 and 8 for physical maps of the United States and the world.

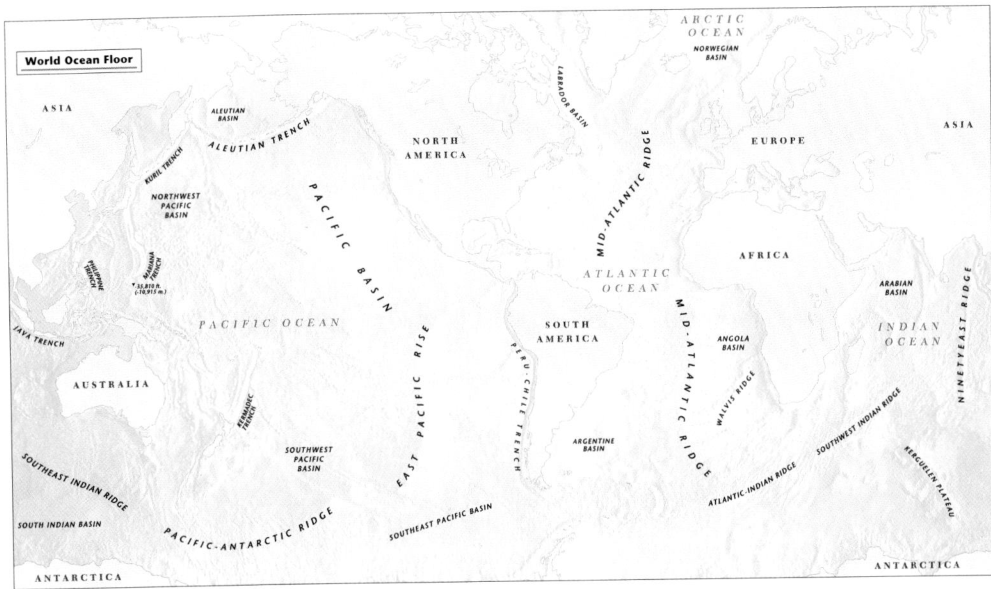


*This physical map shows the structure of the ocean floor.*

## Political Maps

The purpose of a **political map** is to show the political divisions that people have made on the Earth. Political maps show the boundaries of nations and states and the location of towns and cities. We use political maps to locate places where people live and to understand how human beings have divided up the Earth. See Volume 2 for United States political maps and Volumes 5, 6, and 7 for world political maps.

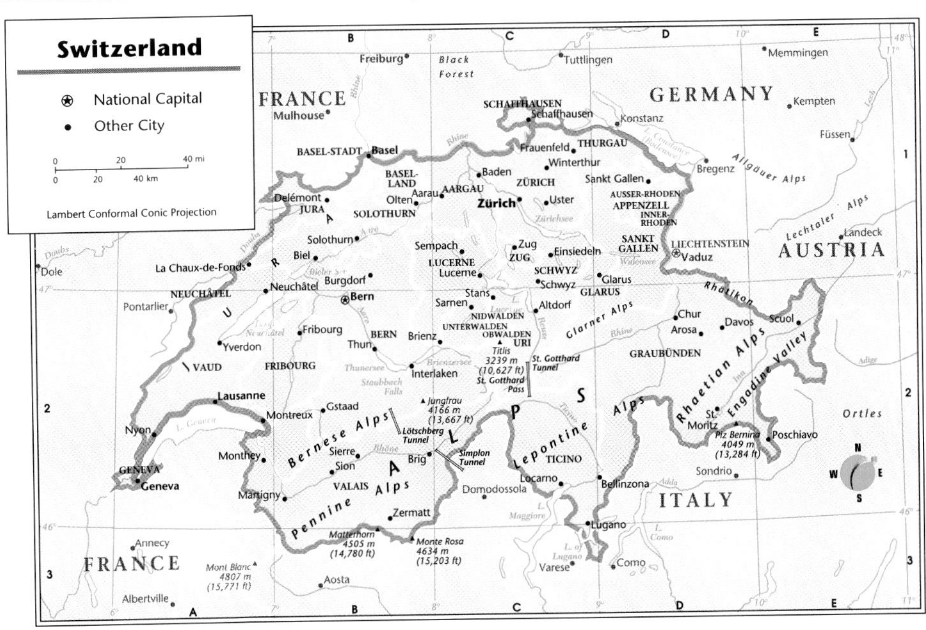


*This political map shows the nation of Switzerland. Boundaries of nations and of Swiss cantons can be found on this map. Capitals and other cities are also found here.*

## Special Purpose Maps

A **special purpose map** focuses on a particular kind of information. Special purpose maps can show physical information such as where a certain crop is grown or what the weather is like in different places. See Volumes 3 and 8 for other special purpose maps of the United States and the world.

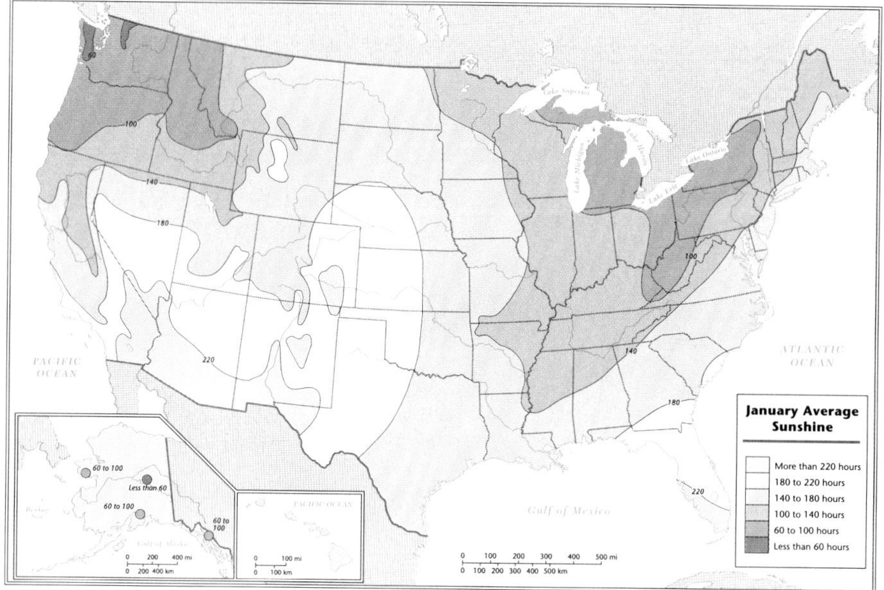


*This map provides information about the amount of sunshine that different parts of the United States receive in the month of January.*

**The title and map key are important guides to understanding a special purpose map. Write a title and design a map key for a special purpose map to show the languages spoken in your community.**

Other special purpose maps show cultural information, information about ways of life. A map can tell you what languages people speak in different places, what religions they practice, what kinds of jobs they have. See Volumes 4 and 9 for cultural maps of the United States and the world.

*This map shows where major religions are practiced throughout the world.*

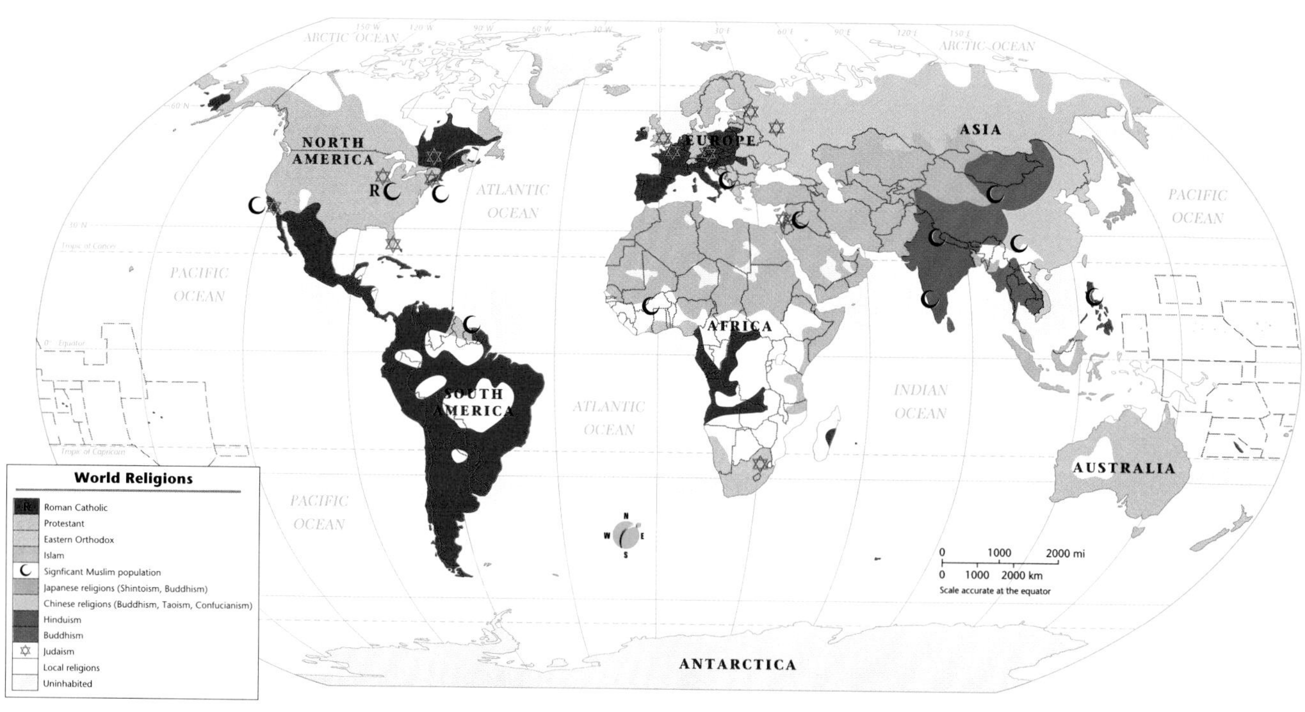

## Historical Maps

An **historical map** can show a moment in time or change over time. Historical maps open a window onto the past. They can show physical information—fertile land that once existed where now there are deserts. They can show political information—the location of cities and kingdoms in ancient times. And they can show cultural information—where people once spoke Latin or where the largest castles were built. See Volume 10: *U.S. and World History Atlas* for more historical maps.

**The Spread of Printing in Europe**

Printing Centers Established

- ● 1448–1475
- ▲ 1476–1500
- ○ After 1500

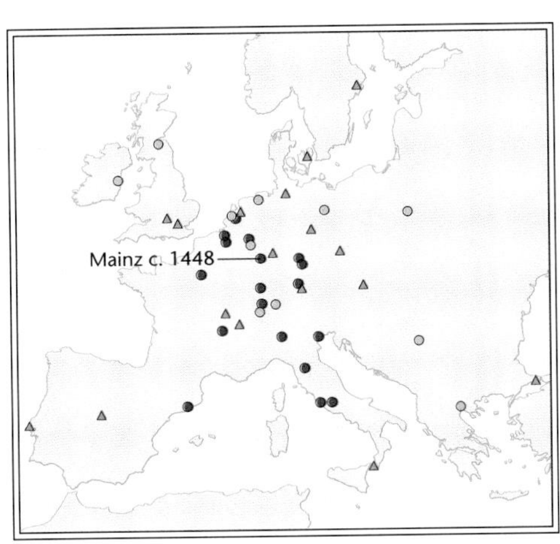


*This map is an example of an historical map that shows cultural information. The theme of the map is the spread of printing technology through Europe in the early Renaissance.*

*This series of historical maps shows the political changes that happened during the settlement and development of the country of Australia. The boundaries of the Australian states and territories changed several times in the past.*

**Growth of Australia**

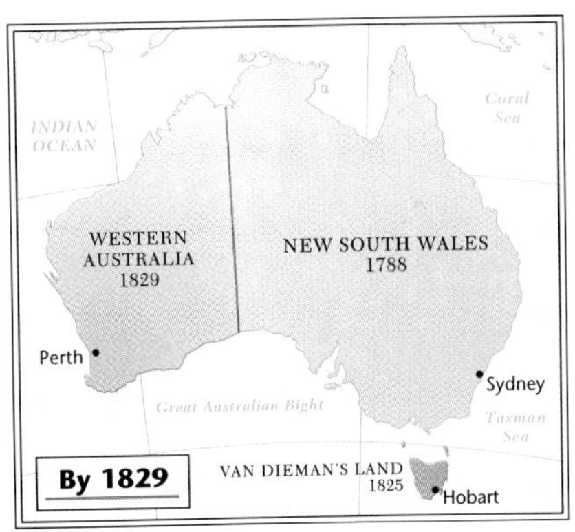


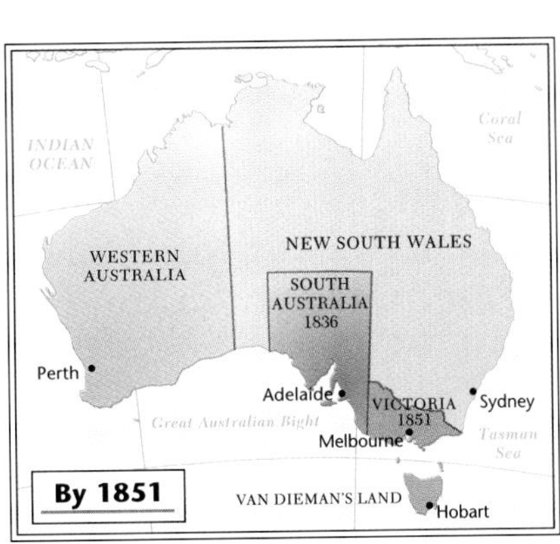


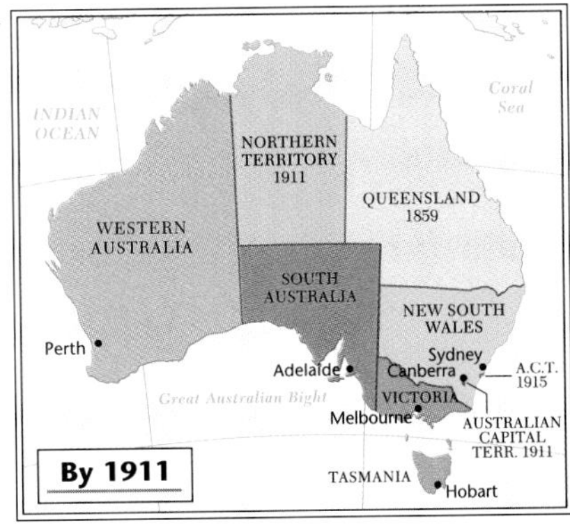

# Map Scale

Maps do not show size and distance exactly as they are on the Earth. To show real size and distance, a map would have to be as large as the part of the Earth it shows. Maps are much smaller than the places they show. For example, three accurate maps of Washington, D.C., fit on the following page. A map that showed the true size of the nation's capital would need 69 square miles of paper!

The size of the real land is reduced to be useful and to fit on paper. The scale of a map shows how much the Earth's surface has been reduced. Scale is the ratio, or relationship, between the real distance on the Earth (ground distance) and the corresponding distance on the map.

$$\text{Map Scale} = \frac{\text{Map Distance}}{\text{Ground Distance}}$$

## Types of Map Scales

**Bar Scale**
Almost every map has a **bar scale** that can be used for measuring. It shows the relationship between map distance and ground distance visually.

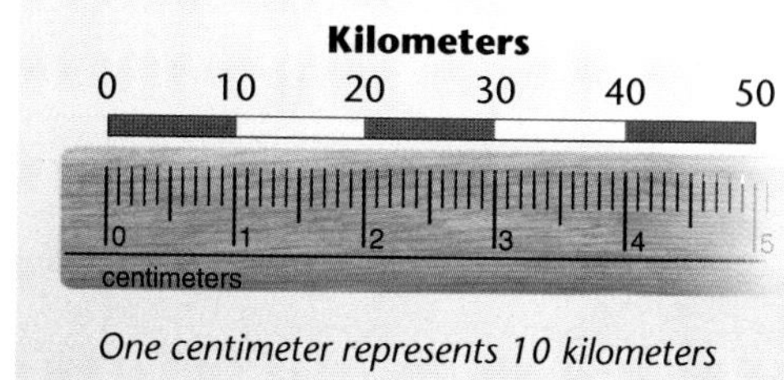


One centimeter represents 10 kilometers

*Expressed as a representative fraction, this scale is 1:1,000,000*

**Verbal Scale**
When a scale is expressed in words, for example, "one inch represents one mile," it is called a **verbal scale.**

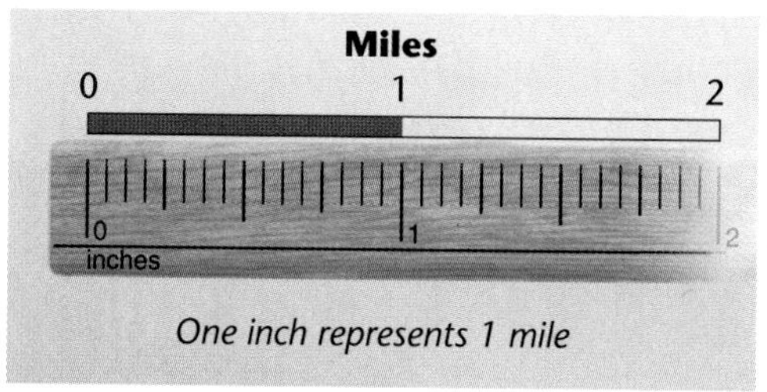


One inch represents 1 mile

*Expressed as a representative fraction, this scale is 1:63,360*

**Representative Fraction**
The scale of a map, expressed as a numerical ratio of map distance to ground distance, is called a **representative fraction.** It is usually written as a fraction such as 1/50,000 or 1:50,000, meaning that one unit of measurement on the map represents 50,000 of the same units on the ground. Therefore one inch on the map would equal 50,000 inches on the ground.

With these scales you can use a map to calculate the size of real places or the distance between real places.

## Changing Scales

The maps on this page show how scale changes when a map's view moves "closer" to or "farther" from the Earth.

*This **large-scale map** (1:50,000) shows a small area such as The Mall in Washington D.C., with a large amount of detail.*

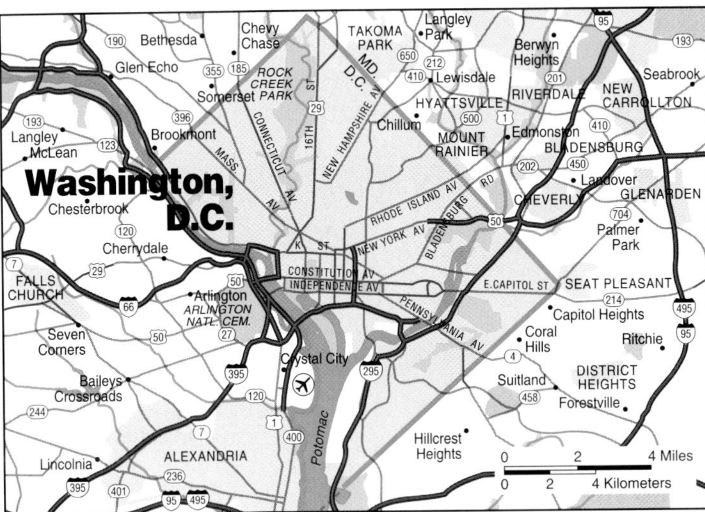


*This smaller-scale map (1:325,000) can show more of the Washington, D.C., area but less detail.*

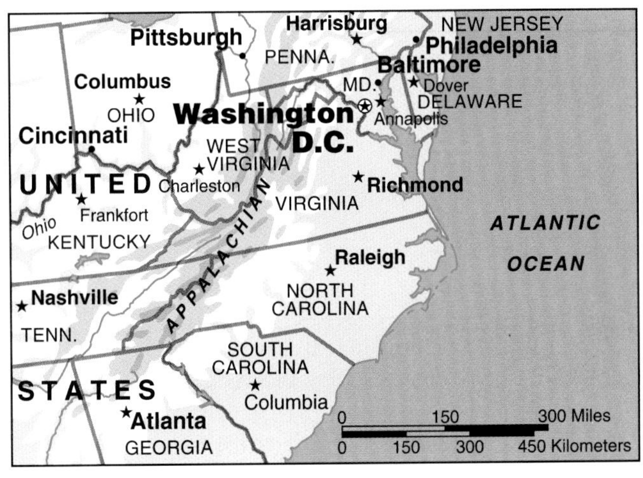


*This **small-scale map** (1:17,000,000) shows a large area such as the mid-Atlantic states, with a small amount of detail.*

The Big Map in Philadelphia is the world's largest map. It is a map of the world measuring 70 feet by 35 feet and is drawn at a scale of 1:2,000,000. Does Washington D.C., appear larger on the Big Map or on the map on this page drawn at a scale of 1:325,000?

Answer: Washington, D.C., appears larger on the map drawn at a scale of 1:325,000 than on the Big Map.

# Latitude and Longitude

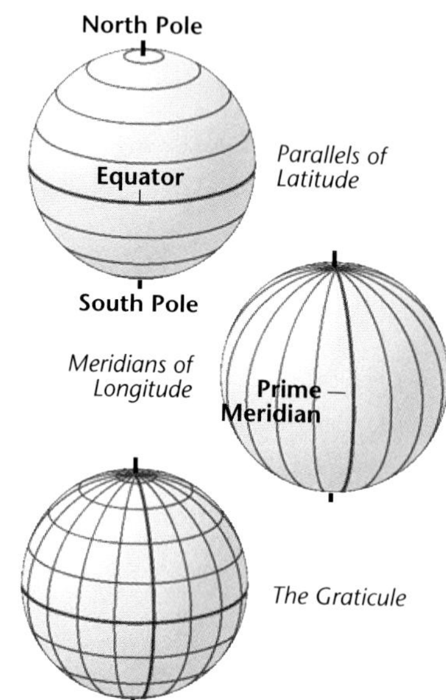


Since ancient times, mapmakers, geographers, and navigators have worked to develop a system for accurately locating places on the Earth. On a sphere, such as the Earth, there are no corners or sides, no beginning or end. But since the Earth rotates on an axis, there are two fixed points: the North Pole and the South Pole. These points make a good starting place for a system of imaginary lines.

These imaginary lines form a grid over the Earth, allowing us to pinpoint the exact location of any spot on the Earth. This spherical grid is called the **graticule.** It is formed by lines called **latitude** and **longitude.**

## Latitude

Halfway between the poles the equator circles the globe in an east-west direction. Latitude is measured in degrees north or south of the Equator, which is 0 degrees (°). Lines of latitude are called **parallels** because they circle the globe parallel to the Equator. Parallels are numbered from 0° at the equator to 90°N at the North Pole and 90°S at the South Pole.

North Pole 90°N
60°N 60°N
30°N 30°N
90° 30°
Equator 0° 0°
90°
30°S 30°S
60°S 60°S
90°S South Pole

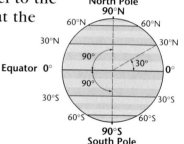

## Longitude

Running from pole to pole, lines of longitude—called **meridians**—circle the globe in a north-south direction. As in any circle or sphere, there are 360 degrees (°) of longitude. The meridians are numbered from the Prime Meridian which is labeled 0°. Meridians east or west of the Prime Meridian are labeled E or W up to 180°. The International Date Line follows the 180° meridian, making a few jogs to avoid cutting through land areas.

180°
150°W 150°E
120°W 120°E
90°W 180° 90°E
90°
60°W 60°E
Prime Meridian
30°W 0° 30°E

Mapmakers once placed the Prime Meridian wherever they wanted. The French located it running through Paris; Americans placed it running through Washington, D.C. The confusion ended in 1884 when 25 nations agreed to start numbering east and west from the Royal Observatory in Greenwich, England.

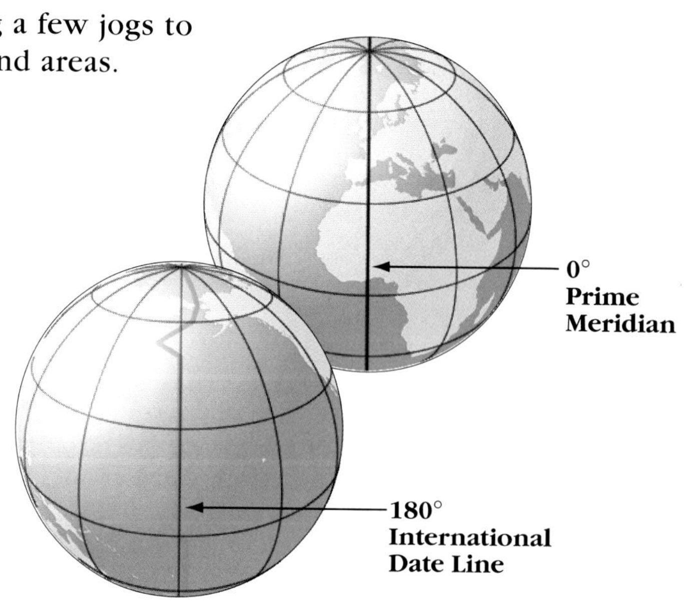

## Parallels and Meridians – the Facts

Parallels

- are lines of latitude used to measure distance north or south of the Equator
- are always the same distance apart (about 70 miles)
- differ in length
- The equator, the longest parallel, is almost 25,000 miles long

Meridians

- are lines of longitude used to measure distance east or west of the Prime Meridian
- meet at the poles
- are all the same length

## Which way north...

North Magnetic Pole
North Geographic Pole
South Geographic Pole
South Magnetic Pole

The geographic North and South Poles are fixed points located at each end of the Earth's axis. The Earth's magnetic fields cause the needle of a compass to point toward magnetic north, not geographic north. The north magnetic pole is located in the Northern Territories of Canada. The south magnetic pole is located near the coast of Antarctica. The magnetic poles are constantly moving.

**Imagine that you started walking from a well-known point on the globe. You walk 1 mile south, turn and walk 1 mile east, and then turn again and walk 1 mile north, ending up exactly where you started! Where are you?**

**Answer: The North Pole**

## Degrees, Minutes, Seconds

A degree (°) of latitude or longitude can be divided into 60 parts called minutes ('). Each minute can be divided into 60 seconds ("). The diagram at right is an example of a place located to the nearest second.

It is written as:
42° 21' 30" N   71° 03' 37" W

- This place is city center, Boston, Massachusetts.

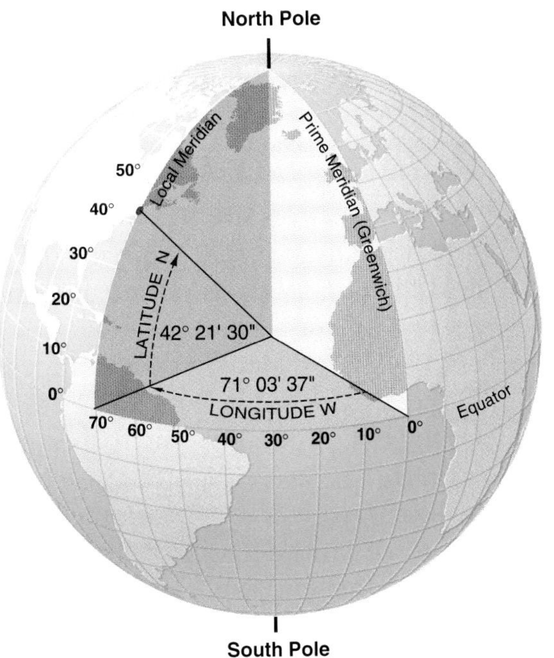

# Map Projections

A globe is the most accurate picture of the Earth as a whole. Only a globe can show distance, direction, and the true shape and area of land and seawater without distortion. But globes do not have some of the advantages of maps. A map can show the whole world at once while a globe must be turned. Maps can be folded up and easily carried. A small map can show detailed information about a small area. To show small details, a globe would have to be enormous. So, for centuries mapmakers have struggled to accurately show a round world on a flat map.

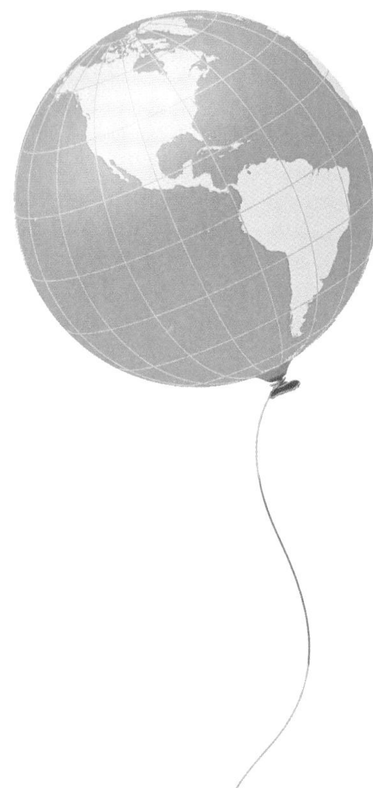

*Imagine the Earth as a large balloon.*

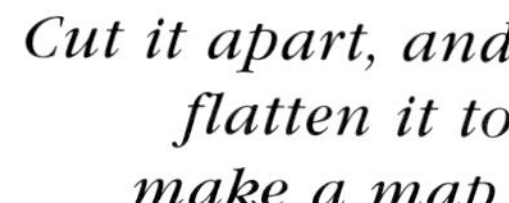

*Cut it apart, and flatten it to make a map.*

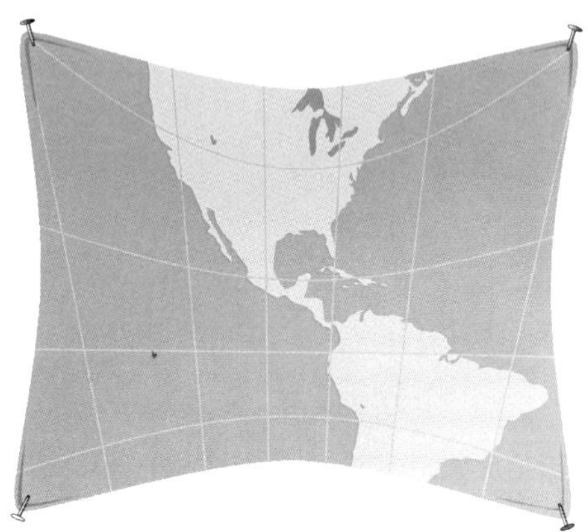

It will be stretched in some places and shrunk in others. To show the round Earth on flat paper, mapmakers use different **projections**, or ways of showing a spherical shape on a flat surface. There are many projections and each has its own strengths and weaknesses.

## Distortion Check List

With every projection the shapes of places are changed somewhat. This is called distortion. To find distortion, you can compare the graticule of a map to that of a globe. (The graticule is the grid formed by lines of latitude and longitude.) On a globe:

- Lines of latitude are parallel
- Parallels are spaced equal distances apart
- The Equator is the longest parallel
- The length of parallels decreases moving toward the poles (which are points)
- All meridians are equal length
- Meridians converge at the poles
- At a given latitude, meridians are equally spaced
- Latitude and longitude meet at right angles

The ways in which the map's graticule differs from this are the areas of distortion on that map.

# Projections – Making the Round World Flat

### Mercator Projection

Gerardus Mercator, a Dutch cartographer, wanted a map that showed direction and shape accurately. Navigators used it to plot their voyages for over 300 years. But the meridians on this projection do not meet at the poles, as they do on the globe. As a result, the lands close to the poles appear much larger than they actually are.

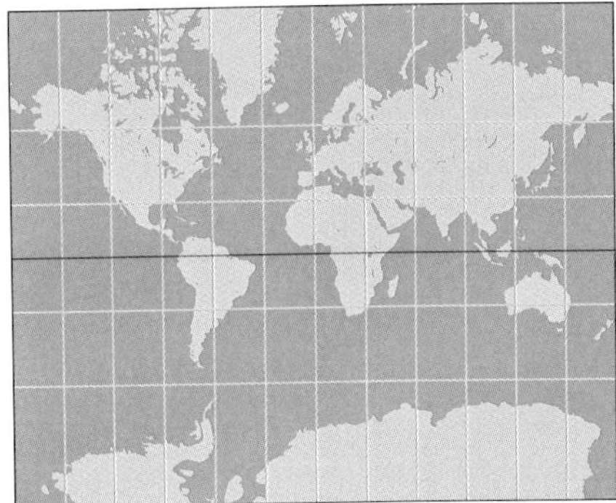

Greenland appears larger than all of South America. On a globe you can see that South America is over nine times the size of Greenland.

A Mercator map distorts distance and size.

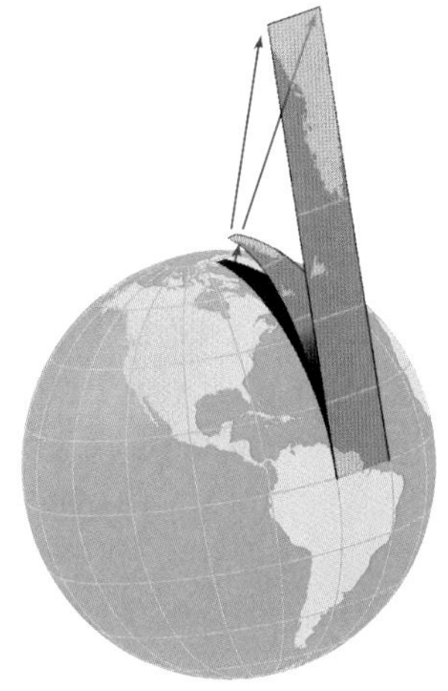

*This diagram shows how a Mercator projection distorts the relative sizes of places. Compare Greenland on the map and the globe.*

### Robinson Projection

Arthur H. Robinson, an American cartographer, wanted to make a map that "looked" right. His projection is used today in many atlases and school books. This map is a compromise that includes every kind of distortion possible on a map: relative size, direction, distance, and shape. But none of the distortions are great. A Robinson map does not distort size as much as the Mercator map, for example.

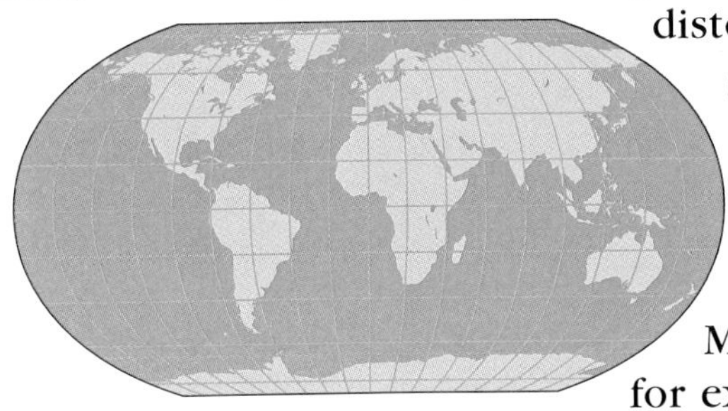

## Choosing a Projection

To choose a projection, mapmakers must ask themselves these questions:

- What information will the map include?
- To show that information, is it more important for the map to show relative size, shape, distance, or directions accurately?
- Would a projection that "looks" right be the best choice?

### Azimuthal Projection

This is an ancient projection that is often used today to show Antarctica or the Arctic. Azimuthal maps show direction accurately. Great Circle Routes (the shortest distance between two points on the globe) appear as straight lines. They also show distance accurately from the center of the map to any point. However other distances, shape, and relative size are distorted.

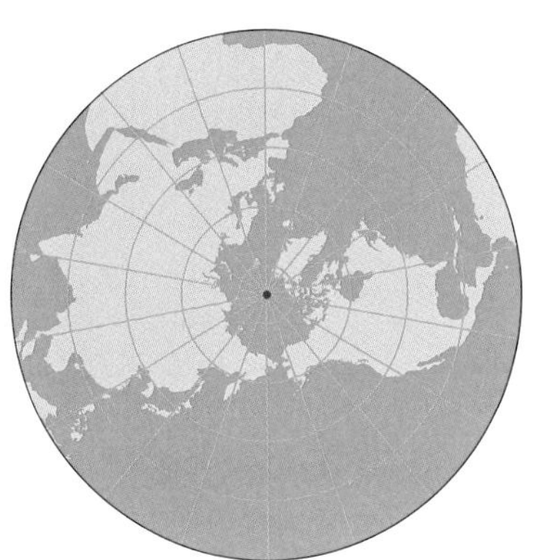

## Map Symbols

Mapmakers, like writers, use symbols to communicate. When a writer puts the symbols h, o, u, s, e, together, we all understand the word house. We understand because the symbols used for writing are standardized. But map symbols are not standard. A blue line may be a river, a road, or the route of a whale swimming in the ocean. On one map dark green may stand for lowlands. On another map it will mean National Park. To unravel the mystery of these symbols, maps come with keys.

## Map Keys

Map keys, also known as legends, are well named because they unlock the meaning of the map's symbols. The symbolic use of color, line, and shapes is easily understood when you consult the key. With a key you can find which boundaries are disputed, where rivers run intermittently, and which waterways are human made. Once unlocked, map symbols can show us places near and far.

**Legend**

- National Capital
- State Capital
- County Seat
- Built-Up Area
- State Boundary
- County Boundary
- National Park
- Other Park, Forest, Grassland
- Indian, Other Reservation
- Military Area
- Point of Interest
- Continental Divide
- Time Zone Boundary
- Limited Access Highway
- Other Major Road
- Highway Shield (90)
- Compass Rose (N, W, E, S)

**Cities**

Type and symbol size indicate population:

| City | Population |
|---|---|
| **Jacksonville** | 500,000+ |
| Tallahassee | 100,000-499,999 |
| Valdosta | 25,000-99,999 |
| St. Augustine | 5,000-24,999 |
| Macclenny | 0-4,999 |

*This is the map key for state maps found in Volume 2:* U.S. Political Atlas.

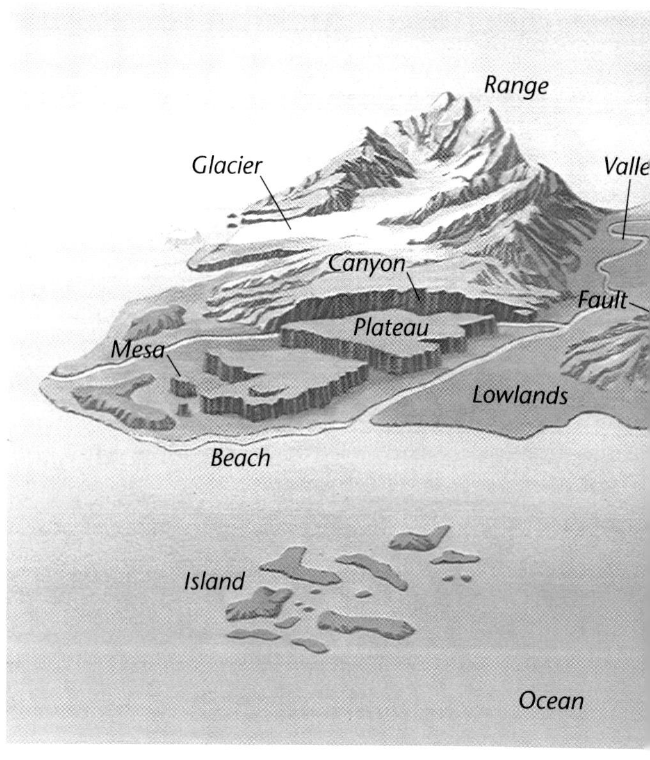


## Geographic Glossary

**basin** A large bowl-shaped depression in the surfac of the Earth.

**bay** A body of water that is partly enclosed by lanc

**beach** Part of a coast or shoreline covered by sand stones.

**canal** An artificial waterway.

**canyon** A deep narrow valley with steep, rocky sid formed by erosion.

**cape** A point of land that extends into a body of water.

**cave** A natural hollowed-out chamber in the Earth, large enough for a person to enter.

**channel** A narrow body of water between two landmasses.

**cliff** A high, steep face of rock.

**coast** Land that borders the ocean, also known as seacoast or seashore.

**continent** Earth's seven great dry landmasses: Asia Africa, North America, South America, Antarctica, Europe, Australia.

**desert** A place that receives less than 10 inches of precipitation a year.

**divide** The boundary or high ground between rive systems.

**dune** A mound or ridge of wind-blown sand.

**elevation** The height of land measured from sea level.

**fall line** A geologic feature where uplands meet lowlands and a series of waterfalls and rapids occur.

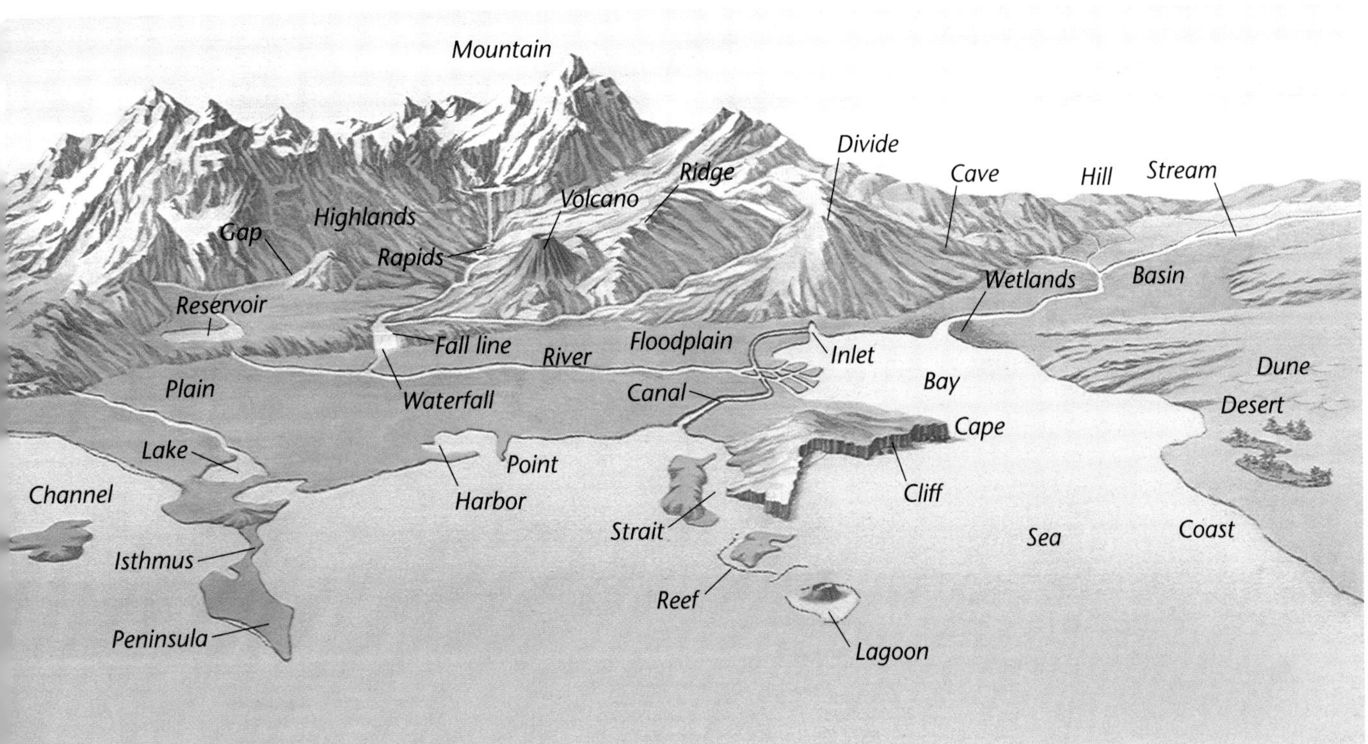


**lt** A break in the Earth's crust caused by vement.

**odplain** A plain bordering the course of a stream t is subject to flooding.

**p** A notch or pass in a mountain range that serves a path through a mountain barrier.

**cier** A huge and slow-moving mass of ice.

**rbor** Any natural or human-made body of sheltered ter deep enough for ships.

**hlands** A mountainous or hilly region.

Elevated land with a rounded summit, smaller n a mountain.

**et** An arm of sea or lake water that reaches inland.

**and** A body of water smaller than a continent and rounded by river, lake, or sea water.

**hmus** A narrow strip of land that joins two large as of land and narrowly separates two bodies of ter.

**oon** Shallow water that is separated from the sea a sandbar, barrier island, or coral reef.

**e** A body of water surrounded by land.

**vlands** Largely flat or gently rolling land that is near level.

**sa** A flat-topped landform with steep rocky slopes all sides.

**ountain** Land rising 1,000 feet or more from the rounding areas, with a wide base and a pointed or rrow top.

**ean** The vast body of salt water that surrounds the ntinents.

**ninsula** A stretch of land that juts out into a lake or ocean and is nearly surrounded by water.

**plain** A broad area of level or gently rolling land.

**plateau** A large elevated area of level or almost level land.

**point** A small cape or the tip of a larger landform that juts out into a river, lake, or ocean.

**range** A long, connected chain of mountains.

**rapids** Fast-flowing section of a river where the riverbed is covered with large rocks and boulders.

**reef** A narrow chain of coral or rock near the surface of tropical seas.

**reservoir** A big, artificial lake where water is stored.

**ridge** A long, narrow stretch of high ground.

**river** A long, large body of water that flows downhill in a natural channel.

**sea** One of the smaller divisions of the ocean, partially enclosed by land.

**steppe** A grassland area covered largely with short grasses.

**strait** A narrow waterway connecting two large bodies of water.

**stream** Any body of flowing water that runs downhill in a natural channel.

**valley** A natural trough between higher ground such as hills or mountains.

**volcano** A vent in the Earth's crust caused by molten rock forcing its way to the surface.

**waterfall** A stream of water that descends suddenly from a higher to a lower level.

**wetlands** An area of land usually covered by shallow water.

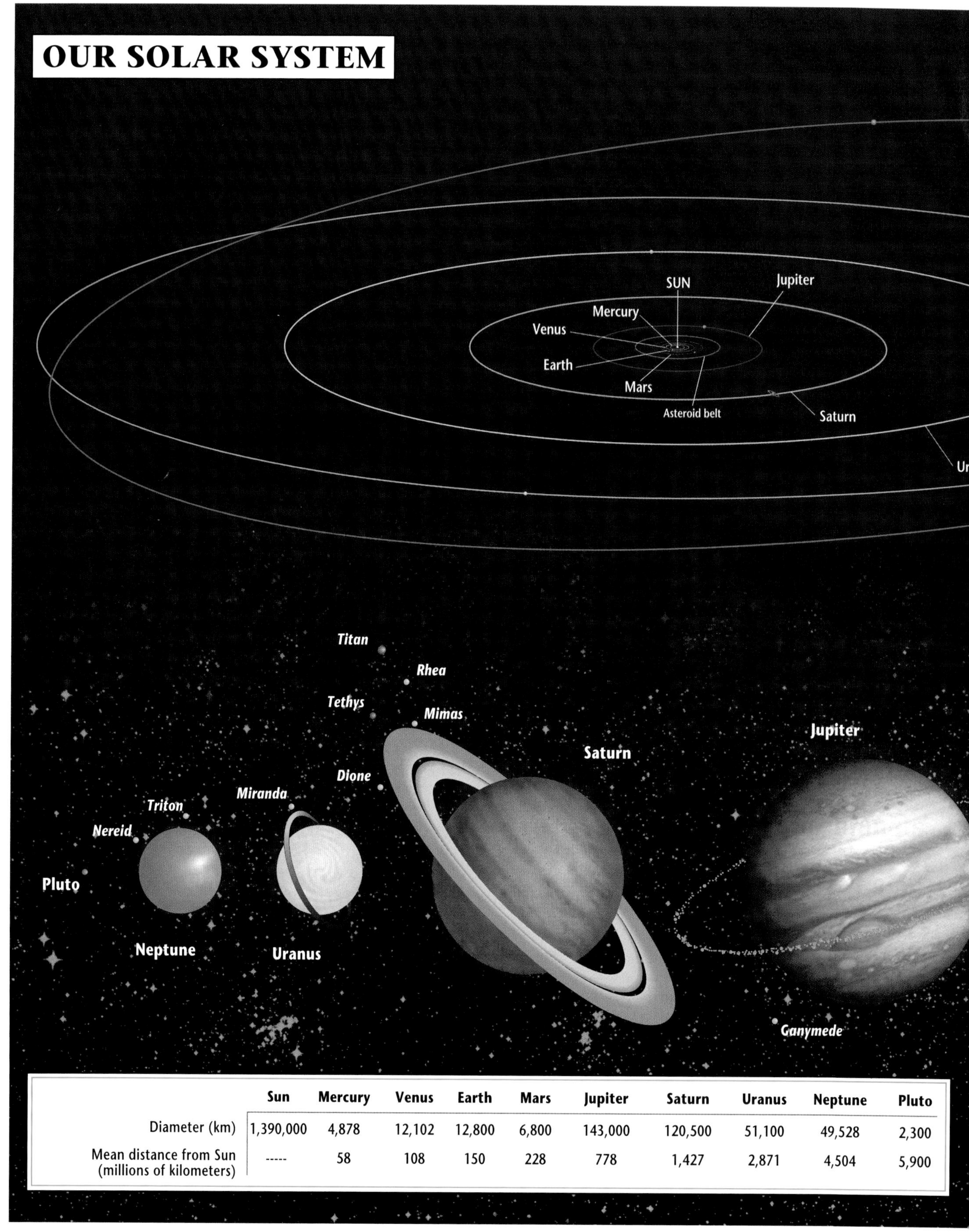


| | Sun | Mercury | Venus | Earth | Mars | Jupiter | Saturn | Uranus | Neptune | Pluto |
|---|---|---|---|---|---|---|---|---|---|---|
| Diameter (km) | 1,390,000 | 4,878 | 12,102 | 12,800 | 6,800 | 143,000 | 120,500 | 51,100 | 49,528 | 2,300 |
| Mean distance from Sun (millions of kilometers) | ----- | 58 | 108 | 150 | 228 | 778 | 1,427 | 2,871 | 4,504 | 5,900 |

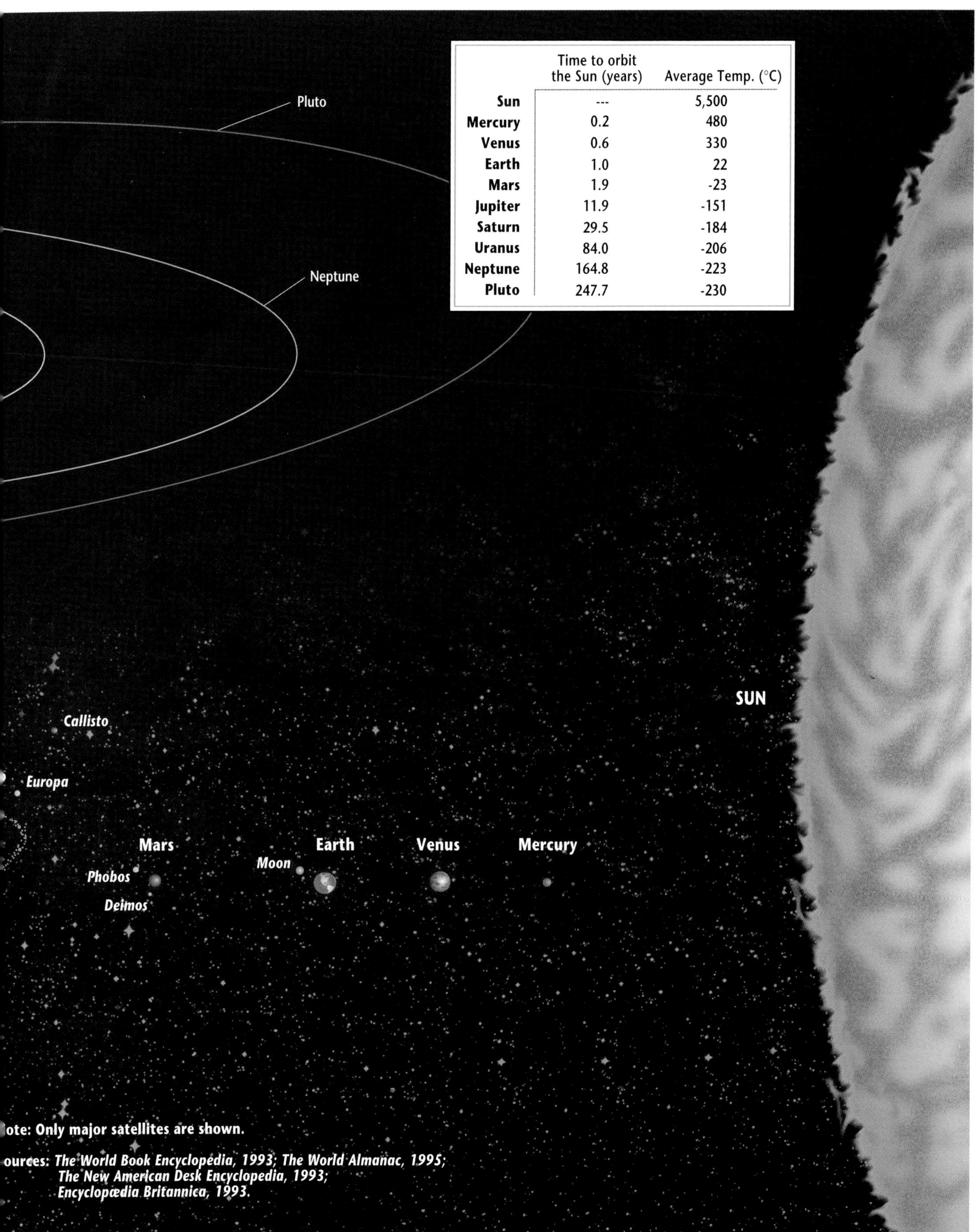


| | Time to orbit the Sun (years) | Average Temp. (°C) |
|---|---|---|
| **Sun** | --- | 5,500 |
| **Mercury** | 0.2 | 480 |
| **Venus** | 0.6 | 330 |
| **Earth** | 1.0 | 22 |
| **Mars** | 1.9 | -23 |
| **Jupiter** | 11.9 | -151 |
| **Saturn** | 29.5 | -184 |
| **Uranus** | 84.0 | -206 |
| **Neptune** | 164.8 | -223 |
| **Pluto** | 247.7 | -230 |

## Our Solar System's Address

The universe is immense. We do not really know how large it is. In it are scattered billions of bright galaxies. They are mysteriously arranged in clusters, as if they are floating on the surface of great empty bubbles. On the edge of one cluster, called the Virgo cluster, is the Milky Way Galaxy. It includes hundreds of billions of stars formed in a loose swirling spiral. Great arms of stars extend 50,000 light years from its star-cluttered center. On an arm called Perseus—30,000 light years from the center—is a star we call the Sun. Within the realm of the Sun's magnetic influence is our solar system.

**What is a light-year?**
**To describe the location or address of our solar system, familiar units of measurements like miles or kilometers are useless. Using units so small would make the numbers too big to write down! Instead, scientists use light-years. One light-year is the distance light travels in one year at a speed of 186,282 miles per second. That is about 6 million million miles per year.**

## Parts of the Solar System

Our solar system can be divided into parts. First are the four terrestrial (earthlike) planets and their moons. They are Mercury, Venus, Earth, and Mars. Beyond Mars is a wide belt of asteroids. These planetlike objects can measure up to 120 miles across, and there are thousands of them. Outside of that come the four giant planets with their moons. They are Jupiter, Saturn, Uranus, and Neptune. Near the outer edge of the Sun's influence is the very small planet Pluto. Comets orbit far beyond Pluto.

*Io, one of the largest moons of the planet Jupiter, is the only place where volcanoes are known to exist besides Earth.*

The solar system also includes chunks of iron and stone called meteoroids, interplanetary dust, and drifting gas called interplanetary plasma.

## How Large...

Although the solar system is immense to us, measured with the speed of light it is less than one light-day (the distance light travels in one day) across.

**Imagine you are on a beach. All around you is sand—billions of tiny grains of sand. Pick one up and imagine that it is the sun. Imagine that all of the grains of sand on all of the beaches of the world are stars. Now answer this question:**

**Are there more grains of sand on the beaches of the world or stars in the universe?**

**Answer: There are more stars in the universe.**

# Index

# Set Index

Volume 1: Glossary of Map Terms
Volume 2: U.S. Political Atlas
Volume 3: U.S. Physical Atlas
Volume 4: U.S. Cultural Atlas
Volume 5: World Political Atlas: Africa and Asia
Volume 6: World Political Atlas: Australia and Europe
Volume 7: World Political Atlas: North America and South America
Volume 8: World Physical Atlas
Volume 9: World Cultural Atlas
Volume 10: U.S. and World History Atlas